ROLAND TERRY

MASTER NORTHWEST ARCHITECT

Justin Henderson

ROLAND TERRY

MASTER NORTHWEST ARCHITECT

UNIVERSITY OF WASHINGTON PRESS

SEATTLE • LONDON

Cover: Roland Terry's former home on Lopez Island. © John
Vaughan, Photographer. © 2000 The Condé Nast Publications Inc.
All rights reserved. Used with permission.
Frontispiece: Roland Terry. Photograph by Robert Pisano. © 1991
The Condé Nast Publications, Inc. All rights reserved. Used with
permission.

Designed by Ed Marquand with assistance by Vivian Larkins
Copyedited by Marie Weiler
Produced by Marquand Books, Inc., Seattle
Printed and bound by C & C Offset Printing Co., Ltd.,
Hong Kong

Unless otherwise indicated all quotations are from conversations
with the author between November 1998 and January 2000.

Library of Congress Cataloging-in-Publication Data
Henderson, Justin.
    Roland Terry : master Northwest architect / Justin
Henderson.
      p.   cm.
   ISBN 0-295-97969-0 (cloth : alk. paper) —
   ISBN 0-295-97970-4 (pbk. : alk. paper)
   1. Terry, Roland—Criticism and interpretation. 2. Architec-
ture, Modern—20th century—Northwest, Pacific. I. Terry,
Roland. II. Title.
NA737.T456 H46 2000
920'.92—dc21   00-027986

Table of Contents

An Appreciation

Jack Lenor Larsen, a nineteen-year-old weaver when he discovered the quiet finesse of Roland Terry's first house, writes an appreciation of his first and frequent client.

To this undergraduate in the years just after World War II, young architects seemed to be knights in shining armor creating Camelot. Of course they were handsome in some way or other, these free souls fighting for the right, for progress, and for fair play. Although they may have been a support group, they were—at least here on the West Coast—individuals. Dragon slayers were they, especially when beaux-arts formalism was ousted for a braver, newer design world. And, after fifteen years of depression followed by years of conflict, people in the Puget Sound area were ready to build houses in keeping with their time.

Modern architecture, together with modern art and design, was a cause to be a part of. Even better, the Northwest Style embraced East Asian aesthetics, Northwest Coast Native American art, and the verdant landscape itself. While the University of Washington enriched its staff with Chinese professors, such painters as Mark Tobey and Morris Graves brought back from Japan a distillation of nature pared to its essence.

At the war's end, Seattle was smug with its high standard of living—with more college graduates and home-owners than anywhere else in the country. Without chronic poverty or minorities, here was the most solidly middle-class city in America. Within it lived a small, evolving group of those not in the middle—including artists, architects, performers, collectors, and a few people of wealth. When those in this elite group felt the need to break with convention, Modernism seemed a reasonable route.

This, perhaps, is just the point. A chief reason Roland Terry was so successful is that he was both an architect and an interior designer. In the third millennium we will realize that even in the 1940s there was sufficient technology to plan a building with the interrelationships of the dwellers uppermost in mind. From human needs and desires spaces can be created, then protected from the elements. In the future, planners will no longer conceive in terms of facades and structure but of people, just as Terry has done for fifty years. No wonder his clients are enthusiastic. Northwest Style—certainly Roland Terry style—is not just rooflines echoing the hills and stained to forest colors. The music is in Terry's orchestration of interior spaces, which dominate in terms of function, natural light, view, and privacy.

While so much of postwar Modernism, especially International Style, has to do with eliminating all elements that might be questionable, including color and pattern, Roland's spaces focused on the pleasures of art, an intimate view, or surprises introduced like grace notes in a musical composition. The attitude was open, generous, and personal.

Perhaps influenced by interior design maven Hope Foote, Terry set out to resolve the challenge of living graciously without staff or formality. His furniture came away from walls to form conversation groupings. Entertaining —even cooking and dining—extended to outdoors, often with the man of the house as chef. Sixty years ago, the concept of bringing the outdoors in and the indoors out was new to us all. Together with a new openness to color, it was a West Coast invention, slowly moving to America's Midwest and East, then changing forever European conventions.

I don't know how the twenty-first century will view this pacesetter and form-giver. So many of his projects have already changed or faded, and his genius for subtlety in juxtaposing surfaces and tonalities never did photograph advantageously. As Hope Foote said, "The best rooms cannot be captured by a camera." So what is left? The remnants of an architectural style or all the good years enjoyed by those living in Terry houses? The memories of thousands of diners of special evenings at the Canlis restaurants or the associations of those who, like myself, recall Roland as a personable, enthusiastic client, and those younger designers and architects who even now consider him their mentor?

Take a moment, then, to speculate just why he was so successful. Admittedly, my analysis is personal and has developed over the decades I have known him. But from our first meeting in 1948, Terry wore his patrician manner (and manners) as comfortably as old shoes. No one ever laughed so often. For Roland, laughter could communicate both approval and a lack of it. "Mr. Terry, do you feel we can bring the job in for one hundred thousand?" In response, his long laugh, meaning, "probably not but do we really need to?"

This easy manner appealed as much to workmen (and my dad, a contractor) as it did to industry captains who became his clients. Terry did not tyrannize his clients but seduced them with visions of a life better—if different—than even their expectations. Fulfilling necessities was never his concern; rather, he wondered what pleasures, what surprises, could be induced? Picture his late 1940s master bedroom with panels that opened wide onto a library. With panels closed, the library became a guest suite. The room was further blessed with a small balcony for admiring the view—checking out the weather or visitors at the front door below.

In a nutshell, what did Roland Terry achieve? If he was too young to invent the Northwest Style first formulated by Pietro Belluschi and John

Yeon, Terry soon became the principal player, with cooperative clients who wanted to be stretched. Some of them offered deep pockets and/or a series of projects.

Philosophic historian Arnold Toynbee wrote convincingly of his theory of great leaders (including Christ and his forty days in the wilderness) being catapulted forward by undergoing a period of withdrawal from society and then returning. Perhaps Terry's withdrawal-return pattern fed his creativity and prolonged his youthful vision. First, after graduation, was his extended tour of Latin American architecture. Later, his two moves away from Puget Sound to search for the freer expression of a painter were complete withdrawals. More severe than sabbaticals, his exits and returns may account for Terry's long youth and his ability to maintain perspective on what was vital and durable.

Jack Lenor Larsen
November 1999

Part I

NORTHWEST MASTER

ROLAND TERRY

INTRODUCTION

Like many recently arrived Seattleites, when I first encountered Roland Terry's architecture, I knew little about his work and even less about his life and times. In the New York architectural circles where I once moved, he was one of half a dozen Seattle architects whose names were bandied about as icons of the "Northwest Style," which was, in truth, an appealing but rather nebulous concept to most New Yorkers. Then, not long after moving here in the early 1990s, I had dinner at Canlis Restaurant, that upper-crust bastion of fine dining that has delighted Seattle gourmets for half a century now. Not least among the charms of Canlis is the room itself, a magnificent, spacious volume suspended on the edge of the cliff off Highway 99, high above Lake Union. Along with culinary pleasures, the restaurant offers one of the most dramatic views in all the Northwest; a view not only unencumbered by the architecture but quietly enhanced and deepened by it, for it simply gets out of the way. An imaginative response to a difficult site, the building features great expanses of angled glass that provides panoramic views, and rugged, natural materials like stone and wood worked into a timeless, subtle design. Canlis, created in collaboration with partners Robert Tucker and Robert Shields in association with George Wimberly, illustrates quintessential Roland Terry architecture.

This first encounter took place on my tenth wedding anniversary. With us on this date were two New York friends, one a native of Seattle. For him, Canlis represented a homecoming of sorts, for he had celebrated his high school senior prom night at Canlis, in 1963. Although it had been

OPPOSITE: The entry to Roland Terry's current residence in Washington State's Skagit Valley (see pp. 128–31) features signature Terry elements, including trellises and extensive plantings that shape a kind of outdoor room and a metal-clad front door. Photo: © 2000 Donna Day

Sweeping expanses of glass typify Terry's designs. Glowing like a welcoming lantern, Canlis Restaurant, built in the late 1940s, remains a successful restaurant after more than fifty years (see pp. 26–27).

redecorated several times between 1963 and 1993, my friend remembered the room to be exactly as we found it thirty years later. This is what is meant by "timeless" design.

Every great architect offers an original vision, one that synthesizes and then transcends all that he or she has learned. Roland Terry's career follows that archetypal mode, yet Terry occupies a unique place in the Northwest architectural tradition. The elements that define his originality are subtle, a fusion of classic Northwest Modernist traditions leavened with a warm yet cosmopolitan sophistication, one that grew organically out of his education, his background in the thriving Seattle art and architecture communities of the 1930s, 1940s, and 1950s, and his experiences while traveling and living abroad. His ability to see the whole picture, to envision a complete design embracing site, building, and interiors—landscape design, architecture, and interior design, to name the basic disciplines—remains unique to this day in the Northwest. Couple that singular talent with a rigorous attention to detail and a remarkable ability to integrate art into architecture—and you have an American original of the Northwest genre.

Local architects who admire Terry's work point to Frank Lloyd Wright as another twentieth-century American architect graced with a similar "big picture" talent. Although Terry never designed buildings on the scale of Wright's later museums, offices, and other institutional structures, on the basis of residential work alone the comparison holds. However, Terry's matchless skill at integrating his ideas with the needs of his clients, particularly with regard to interior design, puts him in a different realm than Wright, who tended to impose his vision on his clients. Terry's body of residential work perhaps includes nothing so renowned as Wright's Fallingwater, but there are numerous Terry houses in the Seattle area (especially his own house on Lopez Island in the San Juans) and elsewhere that illuminate the subtle depth, power, and *completeness* of his design talents. As is evident in the pages that follow, these are houses made for the ages.

This is not to suggest that Terry's commercial work pales in comparison. On the contrary: from the earliest incarnations of Seattle's Canlis Restaurant in the late 1940s through the myriad restaurants, shops, hotels, and offices designed in the 1950s, 1960s, and 1970s, Terry and his shifting cast of partners and associates created a striking and original body of institutional buildings and interiors. While most have fallen victim to alteration or destruction, many continue to thrive in restored, expanded, or renovated form, including Seattle's Canlis, the original Nordstrom flagship store in downtown Seattle, the Half Moon Hotel in Montego Bay, Jamaica, the Kahala Hilton (now Mandarin Oriental) Hotel in Honolulu, and the Halekulani Hotel, also in Honolulu and recently ranked the number one hotel in a *Gourmet* magazine readers' poll. A number of these groundbreaking commercial projects have been included here to illustrate the remarkable diversity of architectural and decorative approaches that Terry and his partners and associates employed in creating comfortable, user-friendly restaurants and other public buildings. As is true with his residences, Terry never chased fads or trends in his commercial designs. Instead he sought the timeless, essential, and complete response to the given design problem—and he did so with subtlety and style.

In recent years, architects and the critics and journalists who write about architecture have chronicled the lack of defining trends in the field. Talented designers continue to turn out great buildings, but there is nothing like Modernism, Post-Modernism, Deconstructivism, or any other dominant movement or design trend on the radar screen. For better or worse, there's a sense that anything goes—as long as it sells.

The Jarvis house features such signature Terry elements as peeled logs, but the interior brick represents an unusual yet practical response to the needs of a family home on a lakefront site (see pp. 48–51).

Reasons for this lack of a "movement" are many and complex, but Anne Gould Hauberg, a dedicated supporter of architecture and the arts, and a long-time friend, admirer, and client of Terry, obliquely suggests one reason when she talks about how Terry designed houses that created a "background for being human." This may sound simple, but the essential rightness of his houses has to do with his ability to create a civilized atmosphere, conjured out of right proportion, the integration of multiple generations of objects and artworks, and a kind of balanced eclecticism. Many contemporary architects lack the depth of learning or culture, the worldliness, to create such civilized places. And so they strain for effect.

Jack Lenor Larsen, one of the great textile designers of the twentieth century (and a Seattle native who often collaborated with Terry) offers his view of Terry's work, placing him in the stream of the Northwest tradition:

Influenced by John Yeon and [Pietro] Belluschi, Terry developed the Northwest house, with low-pitched roof-lines influenced by the shapes of the hills, and by Japanese houses; these Terry houses had lots of terraces, and glass walls, a new trend in a region that had previously sought a sense of enclosure. They also had a kind of reticence, with toned-down colors, fitting into the landscape. You often don't see his houses until you're in them, and this approach to placing the house in the landscape had a tremendous influence on subsequent Northwest design. Also, with interior designer and teacher Hope Foote, Terry began grouping furniture in a completely different way, for conversation, and leaving it there rather than along the walls in the old Georgian style. In this respect the West Coast led the way: the mix of furniture, art and color that was American Modernism began as a Pacific Rim idea; it came from California and the Northwest, then moved to New York, and from New York to Europe.

According to Larsen, then, the direction of influence moved from west to east instead of east to west, with sophisticated New York and even more sophisticated Europe taking their cues from the West Coast, where designers like Terry, having done their traveling and soaked up all the necessary historical influences, then turned around and made something new. And yet this new West Coast style—Larsen wasn't joking when he called it "residential design for a lifestyle without servants," thereby perhaps suggesting what much of this century's best design has been about—drew on plenty of "old" ideas for its richness. Poised between modern functionalism and rich traditionalism, Roland Terry's work embraced the best of old and new.

Given Terry's long and eventful career, which spanned more than half a century, the simplest path to describe his oeuvre is a chronological one. And so we begin in Seattle, in 1917. Those of us familiar only with the big, somewhat boisterous Seattle of the last decade can only dream of what a beautiful small city it must have been eighty years ago, surrounded by seemingly endless miles of virgin forest, snow-covered mountains, and the moody, misty islands and salmon-rich waters of Puget Sound.

Roland Terry grew up in Kansas City, Missouri, an elegantly planned Midwestern city graced with world-class museums, wide, attractive boulevards, and beautifully landscaped parks. His father, Clyde C. Terry, a marine and diesel engineer, piloted ships across the North Pacific from Seattle to

As is evident in this 1950 self-portrait, Terry's talents went beyond architecture into the realm of the fine arts. He grew up in the Seattle arts community of the 1920s and 1930s.

Japan and also invented specialized valves for diesel engines. He died before Roland turned two, and to make ends meet, Roland and his mother moved in with his aunt and uncle, Kittena and William Ingham, and their two boys.

Some summers, the family would join the exodus of people heading north to escape the Kansas City heat and stay with relatives in Seattle. Terrys and Inghams would all pile into a huge old Lincoln touring car and head out, stopping along the way at places like Yellowstone National Park. These cross-country drives exposed Terry at an early age to the grandeur of the American landscape.

From childhood on, he recalls that he always drew and painted, especially pictures of houses. His mother was friendly with Mark Tobey and other artists and was immersed in the lively Seattle art scene of that era, so Terry grew up in an aesthetically informed, arts-conscious environment. He was one of those lucky, gifted children who know what they want to do in life and have the opportunity and skill to do it.

Terry entered the University of Washington School of Architecture in 1935. The UW architecture program had emerged under the leadership of the highly regarded Seattle architect Carl Gould, a graduate of Harvard and a postgraduate student at the Ecole des Beaux-Arts in Paris. Gould arrived in Seattle in 1908. By 1915 he had formed a partnership with Charles Bebb, and the firm received the commission to create a master plan for the University of Washington campus. The plan they initiated is still more or less in place today, as are the eighteen campus buildings they designed, including the striking neo-Gothic Suzzallo Library. Gould also founded the UW School of Architecture (now the College of Architecture and Urban Planning) and chaired it from 1915 until 1926.

Given the dominating presence of Gould, the school in its first decades was known primarily for teaching the beaux-arts style. In the late 1930s and through the war years, under the influence of returning graduates such as Paul Thiry and Paul Hayden Kirk, the architecture school would be transformed by the growing prominence of the stripped-down "form follows function" International Style, or Modernism, elucidated in Europe by Le Corbusier, Mies van der Rohe, Walter Gropius, and others. Roland Terry's university education dovetailed neatly with this 1930s period of transition, when the new wave of Modernists were still willing to embrace the finer or more useful aspects of traditional design. Later, a more rigid Modernist ideology would not permit such an integration of the old into the new, but at this time it seems that many architects and professors sought to create a regionally based design ethos that combined Modernism, especially modern technology, with elements of a more traditional architecture.

The University of Washington teachers who had the greatest influence on Roland Terry were two whose names are now synonymous with this rich, exploratory transitional period: Lionel H. "Spike" Pries and Hope Foote. In their distinctive ways, Pries and Foote promoted a design philosophy that saw no need for a boundary between new and old or for one between interior and exterior. Both were deeply influenced by the natural beauty of Seattle and the Northwest yet were steeped in the wider world they had experienced. In light of Roland Terry's devotion to complete, fully integrated design, it is important to note that Spike Pries was an architect, while Hope Foote was an interior designer who led the UW interior design program, a groundbreaking course that in its time helped shape that profession. Terry's most profound educational experiences came from those separate worlds and from teachers who sought to bring them together.

Born in San Francisco in 1897 and educated in California, Pennsylvania, and abroad, the worldly, sophisticated Lionel H. Pries arrived in Seattle in 1928 following a few years of architectural practice in San Francisco. In Seattle, he formed a partnership with William Bain and began teaching part-time at the University of Washington. After a two-year stint as director of the Seattle Art Institute, he became a UW assistant professor, and in 1932 he became a full-time instructor. As a teacher, he was demanding yet devoted to his best students and profoundly influential, as noted by Drew Rocker in his essay on Pries in *Shaping Seattle Architecture:* "For many young, provincial Washingtonians, [Pries] provided an introduction to a larger world, which encompassed foreign travel, classical music, art history, crafts, and fine arts as well as architecture. For many students from the 1930s to the 1950s (including Victor Steinbrueck, Minoru Yamasaki, Roland Terry, Paul Kirk, Fred Bassetti, Keith Kolb, Wendell Lovett, Astra Zarina, and others), Pries was the center of the of the school."[1]

On a more specific note, Roland Terry, a prize student and a friend, describes Pries thusly, some fifty-eight years later: "Spike was very, very fine with a pencil. He made great sketches, and he knew what he was drawing. He thought designers should make complete buildings, with the inside and outside linked and integrated." Terry also recalls Pries's interest in the Orient —an interest stimulated by his father, who collected Asiatica to furnish a store in San Francisco. That Asian influence subtly permeates much of the best Northwest design, including the work of Roland Terry. And Pries's cosmopolitanism informs the elegance with which Roland Terry always infused his designs.

Most interior designers in the Seattle area credit Hope Foote with creating, or at least defining, what has come to be recognized as the Northwest

1. Jeffrey Karl Ochsner, ed., *Shaping Seattle Architecture: A Historical Guide to the Architects* (Seattle: University of Washington Press, 1994), p. 228.

As shown in the Day house in Oregon (see pp. 52–55), Terry's houses always embrace the outdoors. In addition to creating indoor-outdoor living spaces, they were designed to enhance views.

palette in interior design. Designer Allen Vance Salsbury studied with Foote and later worked with Roland Terry on a number of projects. Of Foote, Salsbury said, "She had a great sense of the region, and she developed the Northwest palette. And as a teacher, she gave her students inspiration, and was in turn inspired by them." According to Warren Hill, another Seattle industrial and interior designer who studied with Foote and worked with Roland Terry, Foote's approach to design was concerned "with the human use of space, and the use of natural materials." Hill describes Foote as having been deeply influenced by Ken Weber, a designer who had left the atelier of Josef Hoffman in Vienna to work in Los Angeles, and by the California followers of Frank Lloyd Wright. These influences thus tie the roots of modern Northwest design into the progressive design traditions of Europe and California.

Of course, in Seattle these traditions took another direction, influenced as they were by the moody green landscapes and seascapes of Puget Sound, and those lands across the Pacific—especially Japan—that share the same organic, evocative palette. The region's developing design idiom came to include great expanses of glass to frame and reveal the compelling Northwest vistas and to deliver as much of the elusive Northwest light as possible; interiors and exteriors shaped and colored by native plantings; rough stone; unpainted or naturally stained wood, often in its most fundamental form, the peeled or driftwood log; and fabrics and finishes in colors and textures that echo and enhance those natural materials.

Hope Foote directed the University of Washington's interior design program—a groundbreaking entity in that it was one of the few independent, university-level interior design offerings in the country—from 1923 to 1967. Thus in the 1930s Roland Terry had the good fortune to study interior design with Foote as an integral if separate part of his architectural schooling. As Warren Hill noted in an essay written for a book on designer Jean Jongeward (another great admirer of and collaborator with Roland Terry), "Foote encouraged her students toward unpretentiousness, an attitude that made the usual historically oriented approach to the forms, surfaces, and volumes of interior design seem inappropriate. Her simplified spaces and furnishings addressed function and form in a poetic response; furnishings echoed the planes of walls, floors, and ceilings. By focusing attention on functional built-in storage she made the usual freestanding storage pieces, so important in earlier periods, no longer necessary."[2] And as noted earlier by Jack Lenor Larsen, Foote, along with Roland Terry, developed the idea of grouping furniture to abet conversation—an idea that in retrospect seems simple and obvious, but one that quietly helped change the course of interior design history.

THE EARLY YEARS

After graduating from the University of Washington with a Bachelor of Architecture degree in December 1940, Terry went to work for Seattle architect Lister Holmes, for whom he had interned summers while in school. After less than a year in Holmes's office, Terry was honored with an American Institute of Architects (AIA) Langley Scholarship, and in October 1941 he headed to San Francisco, the starting point for an extended trip to South America. His destination was Rio de Janeiro, to study the modern buildings designed by Le Corbusier and his Latin American disciples, such as Oscar Niemeyer.[3]

In Rio, Niemeyer showed Terry around. He recalls, "I saw the best modern buildings. Corbusier did the first high-rise in Rio, the Ministry of Education, which was unusual in that the architect had developed a lighting system that filtered natural light through exterior shutters composed of large

Built-in cabinets, employed here at the Hauberg house in Seattle (see pp. 38–43), eliminate the need for bulky, freestanding storage pieces.

2. Diane Douglas et al., *Jean Jongeward in the Northwest Design Tradition* (Bellevue, Wash.: Bellevue Art Museum, 1995), p. 24.

3. Translating Corbusier's rigid lines and planes into lush, organic curves, in the 1950s Niemeyer would go on to design many of the significant buildings in Brazil's ambitious ode to the International Style, the capital city of Brasilia.

scale vertical and horizontal screens." That very specific recollection points to one of Terry's design strengths: his mastery of light, both natural and artificial, in creating dramatic yet comfortable, user-friendly interiors. Terry's other Latin American recollection makes a telling counterpoint: he spent some time (including a stay in a hotel built in the sixteenth century) at Cuzco and Machu Picchu, Incan cities high in the Peruvian Andes, and enthusiastically remembers "the wonderful stonework—how the stones fit together so perfectly," in the roads, walls, and buildings of those ancient places. Another Terry strength is thus anecdotally illumined: his devout attention to detail. As Mies van der Rohe famously put it, "God is in the details." Roland Terry clearly appreciated and understood the truth of that remark and how well it applied to the great designers of antiquity as well as to the great Moderns.

Terry returned to the United States in May 1942 and soon began a four-year stint in the military. During his tour of duty he spent time in Hawaii, the western Pacific, and New Mexico, a place that made a powerful impression on him, particularly the strikingly beautiful high-desert terrain around Santa Fe. The area is more settled now, but in the 1940s the Native American presence surely was stronger, the land wilder. Terry has been back many times, and even now, comfortably retired in his Skagit Valley home, he devours the novels of Tony Hillerman, set on the Navajo and Hopi Reserva-

At the Hauberg house on Bainbridge Island, Terry demonstrated the art of creating comfortable outdoor rooms that flow seamlessly into adjacent interior spaces (see pp. 60–63).

tions of the Southwest. Hillerman tells a good story, but what draws Terry to the books is the writer's knowledge of the southwestern landscape and his ability to evoke an authentic sense of that powerful area.

In 1946 Terry formed his first professional firm, Tucker Shields & Terry, with former UW schoolmates Robert Tucker and Robert Shields. He stayed with the partnership until 1951. During that five-year period the firm designed a number of custom residences, renovations, and additions in and around Seattle. Tucker Shields & Terry designed their own offices in 1946–47, which were later destroyed.

In 1949 Terry took a leave from his practice and headed for Europe in the first of several sojourns to the Old World. After spending time in Spain and Italy, he traveled to France, where he enrolled at the Académie Julian in Paris. Contrary to what one might expect, Terry did not study architecture, design, or even architectural history. Instead, he pursued the other, perhaps more refined, means of self-expression that had captivated him all his life— he spent the next year studying painting. To go from professional architect in Seattle to art student in Paris suggests a restless, independent, and creative personality, one possibly more interested in things artistic than practical. And in fact, not long after Terry returned to Seattle he left the firm of Tucker Shields & Terry.

In 1952 Terry formed a partnership with Philip A. Moore. During the next decade Terry & Moore completed a large number of residences and commercial projects, establishing Terry as one of the premier architects in the Northwest.

LEFT: In the early 1940s, Terry traveled to South America on a Langley Scholarship. During the trip he produced a series of watercolors.

RIGHT: In 1949 Terry took a leave from his practice to travel and study in Europe. While traveling he kept his eye on the buildings, as in this painting, *Along the Seine.*

The Florence Beach Terry House

ROLAND TERRY EXECUTED HIS FIRST successful residential project between 1935 and 1937, while just a sophomore in architectural school. Displaying precocious self-confidence and a well-developed design sensibility at a remarkably early age, Terry created an innovative, inexpensive house for his mother, Florence Beach Terry. He was eighteen years old at the time he made the design, and thanks to his mother, an accomplished artist and his most avid supporter, he had spent most of his youth immersed in the Seattle art world. An article on the house that was published in a now-anonymous magazine was titled, "What you can learn from custom-built houses." As is evident in the photos, this early project already exhibited many of Terry's architectural trademarks: a well-conceived adaptation to a typical Northwest, i.e. sloping, site, the ingenious use of simple, natural materials in elegant ways, a marvelous sense of spatial relationships, and an almost uncanny ability to integrate interior and exterior harmoniously.

Even now, over sixty years later, the small, flat-roofed house in Seattle's Blue Ridge neighborhood has a clean, modern look to it. Imagine its impact in 1937 and you gain a sense of what an innovator Terry was. He recently said of this house: "I was interested in a simple structure—structure that you could understand. Basically, the house has two blank walls and two window walls, with nothing in the way. It was radical in its time." He credits Spike Pries with helping him, not only in developing the plan, but also by selling him a grid of windows at an economical price. Surrounded and sheltered by lush plantings, especially a magnificent wisteria that softens the edges of the building along the roofline, the comfortable, functional structure is graced with a 14-foot ceiling in the living room that creates a sense of spaciousness

Terry designed this house with its circular view terrace for his mother, Florence Beach Terry, in 1935, when he was eighteen years old.

OPPOSITE: Wisteria frames a generous grid of windows opening onto a sheltered patio of the house.

23

Dearborn-Massar

ABOVE: Draperies divide the dining room from the living room and view terrace beyond.

OPPOSITE, TOP RIGHT: Another view of the living room shows Terry's innovative use of low-cost materials—plaster and pigment finished with beeswax. High ceilings expand the sense of space.

OPPOSITE: Drawing and plan illustrate the sophisticated interplay of interiors and exteriors.

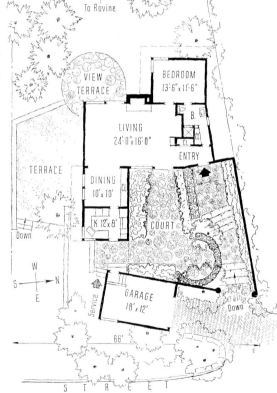

in the 950-square-foot interior. The simple, practical furnishings are positioned to enhance the openness. Low-cost materials include plaster and plywood finished with pigment and beeswax, and an exposed-beam ceiling. The interior plan is basically open: the dining room is separated from the living room with draperies, with the division further indicated by a shift in ceiling height from 14 to 9 feet. The lowered ceiling also helps establish a more intimate mood in the dining room.

The house sits on a sloping site facing west, with the entry to the east. Large grids of window wall—Spike Pries's discount windows put to brilliant use—open the living room to a pair of terraces to the south and west, revealing dramatic views. To provide another outside space with shelter from the prevailing winds, Terry organized the plan so that the kitchen and garage surround a small enclosed courtyard on the east, or street, side of the house, linked to the living room by a bank of windows with a pair of glass doors. This original little house offers a revealing preview of the brilliant work to come.

Canlis Restaurant, Seattle

TUCKER SHIELDS & TERRY, in collaboration with the Honolulu architectural firm of Wimberly & Cook, designed the first incarnation of Seattle's Canlis Restaurant. George Wimberly knew Roland Terry from the University of Washington, so when Wimberly obtained the commission to plan Canlis, he turned to Terry to conceptualize and complete the design. The structure, designed and built between 1949 and 1951, was renovated by Tucker & Shields in 1953, after Terry left the firm, and then revamped again by Terry & Moore in 1958. Recently, in the mid-1990s, Northwest architect James Cutler executed yet another update of Canlis, but through all these remodels, the essence has not changed. The generous volumes, native wood and stone, subtle artwork, and muted tropical Pacific accents that define Canlis's simple, elegant atmosphere remain the same. The sloping glass walls—angled upward and outward to prevent glare from reflected ceiling lights—offer inspired views of the boating activity on Lake Union. The dynamic sense of movement from level to level has not been changed, nor has Terry's compelling sense of how best to experience the subtle variations of sunlight and moonlight in the Northwest sky and water. The way Roland Terry tells it, owner-operator Peter Canlis did miss out on one magical opportunity with the Seattle property: Terry had convinced artist Mark Tobey, then relatively unknown, to do a mural for the upstairs dining room, but Canlis didn't want to spend the money.

Terry's first commercial project, Seattle's still-popular Canlis Restaurant, opened in 1951. The building and interiors have been renovated several times since, but the essence remains the same.

The Burnett/Benditt House

WITH ROLAND TERRY SERVING AS LEAD DESIGNER, Tucker Shields & Terry created the Burnett house in the Washington Park area of Seattle around 1949. The house has belonged to Marcella Benditt since 1976. A number of years ago, in an effort to better organize it for her own needs, she had the house remodeled by Seattle architect David Hewitt. Savvy enough to appreciate the fundamental strengths of the architecture, Benditt and Hewitt altered with a light hand.

Photographs of the Burnett/Benditt house from the early 1950s and 1999 illustrate the enduring strengths of the architecture and interiors. The house stands as a fine example of Terry's talent for meeting the challenges of a difficult site with an imaginative, original response—one that stirred the traditionally minded neighborhood into a bit of a lather back when it was built. Today, the house looks modestly modern, an understated, well-integrated standout in a lovely neighborhood marred of late by a plethora of grandiose faux chateaux and overbuilt contemporary mansions. As David Hewitt himself noted in a recent interview, "This is still a very powerful house, and I loved working on it. You look for buildings like this, that retain architectural clarity without . . . dominating or intimidating the neighborhood."

Terry's solution to the problems posed by the client and the site offers a lesson in turning difficulty into inspiration. The rugged, hilly site, approached by a steep uphill drive, and the client's request for a carport with sheltered access to the front entrance led Terry to an audaciously simple solution: He grounded the main portion of the house—one story with a full basement—at the highest point on the site to reach the views; he then extended a large section of the building on a horizontal plane supported by concrete piers

Terry's solution to the problem of a hilly site for the Burnett house was to extend the house into space and support it on concrete piers. Then and now, stairs lead from the carport up to the front door.

and put the carport underneath. Then, taking this dynamic plan to a more intriguing level, Terry installed a rather grandly scaled stairway that rises from the carport to the front door and foyer. On entry, an unobstructed view across the living room to the left takes in a long seating area beneath a window wall, a wall of greenery, and beyond, Lake Washington. To the right, a long, Japanese-style gallery—glassed in on one side, and thus flooded with soft, natural light—parallels the entry stair and leads back to the master suite above the carport. At the north end, the house floats in the air atop the columns; at the south end, the living room, dining room, outdoor terrace, and kitchen are firmly grounded and buried in a dense garden of rhododendrons and other native plants. To some it looks precarious, but this house isn't going anywhere. Terry recalls that after they had put the supporting columns in, and before they had put the house on top, a fairly strong earthquake struck. The columns wavered slightly, then returned to their original position, solid as ever.

The home is finished both inside and out in a brown and muted moss-green palette. Though surrounded by trees, the house's large window walls admit generous amounts of softly filtered green-tinged light, lending the organic interior a soothing, mellow ambience. The spirit of the house evokes Japan, perfectly suited to showcasing Benditt's collection of Asian art. But even without the artwork, the serendipitous siting, the scale of the rooms, and the expansive windows establish a tranquil, timeless Japanese mood.

View of the extended bedroom wing and the sheltered carport below. The Lake Washington–area home was designed and built in 1949.

OPPOSITE: Views in two directions across the living room to the dining room (top) and the library, formerly the master bedroom, illustrate the simple clarity of the plan, the muted, organic palette, and expansive windows. The house makes a perfect setting for owner Marcella Benditt's Asian art collection.

Remodel of the Paul Roland Smith House

ANOTHER TUCKER SHIELDS & TERRY PROJECT was the expansion-renovation of the Paul Roland Smith family home. Several years later Terry would design a new house for the Smiths, but this earlier project published in *House & Garden* in 1953, serves as an essay in clever, space-wise renovation, in transforming a traditional-looking house—in a tradition-minded neighborhood—into an entirely different kind of home without significantly altering the streetside appearance or the basic floorplan.

In the Smith remodel, Terry began by replacing the east-facing living- and dining-room walls with floor-to-ceiling glass, opening up expansive views of Lake Washington. These glass walls look onto a partially sheltered (with corrugated plastic) outside terrace, finished with brick and tough, durable terrazzo. A sliding glass door links a greenhouse to the adjacent dining room. Behind the greenhouse, a sunny workroom was created to make space for gardening chores. Thus the whole back of the house was opened and expanded outward—with a marble deck for dancing—to embrace the panorama of the lake and the mountains beyond. This openness lends the house a sense of spaciousness and proximity far greater than one would expect of an 80-by-150-foot urban lot, divided from the lake by a street.

On the entry side of the house, Terry created a wood and corrugated-plastic shelter and a new sidelight for the front door. Meanwhile, he closed off two living-room windows to enhance privacy. This created an interior wall large enough to accommodate an antique Japanese screen, an item that Terry had suggested to the Smiths as a focal point for the house. The interior palette, carried out in buckskin walls, a white Indian carpet, and a sofa finished with gold Peruvian linen, was chromatically keyed to this screen,

In his remodel of a house near Lake Washington for the Paul Roland Smith family, Terry installed floor-to-ceiling glass in the living room and dining room, embracing the lake and views.

A partially sheltered terrace makes a fine outdoor room
and strengthens the interior-exterior connection.

presaging Terry's skill at developing designs that integrate individual works of art. Terry also custom-designed several pieces of furniture for the house, including a sideboard and a cabinet finished in rawhide, a rough-sounding material that Terry's skillful design transformed into an elegant, appealing texture. Such exotic finishes, which also included green Guatemalan tile in the greenhouse and a range of fabrics and textiles custom designed by Jack Lenor Larsen, illuminate the architect's willingness to start from scratch with custom work or to shop the world in search of the right piece or element. In 1953, along with the antique Japanese screen, the Smiths displayed a Chinese Tang-dynasty horse, an English copper pot, Japanese lamps, and Terry's custom-designed furniture in a stylish mix. From the street, it didn't appear that much had changed, but the essence of the house and the experience of living in it were radically altered and much improved by Terry's fully integrated approach.

The link between inside and outside dissolves beneath the corrugated-plastic roof sheltering the greenhouse-workroom and the adjacent terrace.

Part II

EMERGING BRILLIANCE

THROUGH THE 1950S TERRY & MOORE'S many successful residential and commercial projects established Roland Terry as a unique design force on the Seattle scene. Terry achieved a reputation as an architect capable of integrating the complex requirements of demanding clients into buildings that also expressed his personal vision.

RESIDENTIAL WORK

As architect Jim Olson, a principal in Olson/Sundberg Architects of Seattle, put it in a 1998 interview, "Roland Terry was the man. For residential design at the highest of the high end, no one else came close. He created an environment, a lifestyle, with a sense of history. It was a very cosmopolitan kind of thing. He was like a high-end interior designer, but also an architect, and so was able to create warm, comfortable, yet architectural environments. I can't think of anyone else who did what he did, wedding European elegance with Northwest Modernism." Seattle architect David Hewitt offers another view of Terry's work: "He was less concerned about formal massing than most architects. He worked from the inside out, doing a series of houses with wonderful interior courtyards, like the Hauberg house [see pp. 38–43], where he was able to create contrasts, of intimate space and great scale." This dramatic, appealing juxtaposition, of intimate garden or courtyard counterpointed by spectacular panoramic view, with the building sited between, is a recurring theme in Terry's residential work.

Terry mastered the art of orchestrating heavy, rough materials like stone and raw logs with surprising grace and delicacy. The counterpoint of intimacy and panorama is another trademark.
Photo: © 1980 Dick Busher

37

The Hauberg Town House

TERRY DESIGNED ONE OF HIS FIRST great houses of the 1950s in 1953–54 for John H. Hauberg Jr. and Anne Gould Hauberg on a steep, difficult site in Seattle's Washington Park neighborhood, overlooking Lake Washington. The aesthetically adventurous, progressively minded Haubergs—he a contemporary art collector and connoisseur, she the daughter of architect Carl Gould and a great admirer and student of architecture and the arts—hired Warren Hill to design furniture and to collaborate with Terry on the interiors. Irene McGowan, who worked on numerous Terry projects, designed most of the light fixtures. The Haubergs also commissioned structurally integrated and/or freestanding artwork from such well-known Northwest artists and artisans as Glen Alps, Guy Anderson, Paul Bonifas, Everett DePen, Morris Graves, Paul Gustin, and Mark Tobey. From Graves, Terry learned a technique for whitening hemlock, the house's primary finish material. Guy Anderson and Anne Hauberg gathered stones from a mountain creek for the Anderson-designed terrace. Hill recalls the project as "a seven-ring circus, with so many people involved." A seven-ring circus, with Roland Terry as ringmaster—for the heart of the matter, the design of the house itself, was his. Terry also created the small, elegant gardens that surround the house and feature a vibrant mix of integral artwork, plantings, and water features.

To better appreciate the groundbreaking quality of this cubist, Northwest International–style house, one need look no further than a *House Beautiful* article published in November 1960, several years after the house was built. At that time, the writer felt compelled to defend the very idea that a house as modern as this could be described as elegant: "This house proves that elegance, whether as an environment or a way of life, does not require

A multilayered box of glass and whitened hemlock, the Hauberg house from the early 1950s remains an iconoclastic piece of architecture to this day. A difficult, hilly site inspired the complex design. Photos: Dearborn-Massar.

Drawing shows the intriguing interplay of horizontal and vertical elements.

OPPOSITE: With their generous expanses of glass, Terry's designs always provide dramatic views.

the trappings of the past. . . . it is a full expression of contemporary design, detailed and furnished only with the skills of today's artists and craftsmen. Yet because of the restraint and finesse used throughout, the result can truly be called elegant in every sense of the word." Elegant, yes, and possessed, notes the writer, of what he calls "a kind of high-level non-conformity, the freedom to choose the best without concern for a particular design dogma." In this case, the description fit both client and architect.

As Anne Hauberg pointed out in a recent conversation, the first challenge Terry faced in planning her home was adapting to the narrow, steeply sloping site, and he responded, she says, "with a brilliant, ingenious plan." The house is distributed over three levels, with the entry foyer (along with garage, child's bedroom and playroom, service kitchen, bath, and storage room) on the lowest level. This entry level links to the street, about 20 feet below, via steps that rise up a slope with multiple landings. From this "ground" floor a spacious stairway with a landing and a turn ("so that people wouldn't get exhausted coming in," recalls Hauberg) leads up to the double-height main living level. The turns in the stairway also assure a dramatic moment of entry, when the overscale main volume opens to view. From there an enclosed stairway leads to the uppermost level housing the master suite as well as three children's bedrooms.

The multilevel floorplan is highly ingenious, but for Terry, it was a means rather than an end. Along with the brilliantly integrated artwork, what elevates the house into the inspired realm are the inviting, open-space plan of the main level (overlooked by a mezzanine on the upper level) and the magnificent double-height window walls, which provide panoramic views from the main living level and the master suite (a sliding screen allows privacy in the master-suite bedroom). Like many of Terry's rooms, the experience of being in this one is profoundly intensified by its relationship to the exterior. A second double-height window wall links the living room level to an art-filled "adult" terrace on the west or back side of the house—an intimate counterpoint to the territorial lake view. On the lowest level, a second terrace provides children with an outdoor play area, maximizing the use of available space.

The photographs here illustrate the rich selection of artwork, unusual finishes, and custom-designed furniture and carpets by the various artists, artisans, and designers. Less obvious are the custom-designed light fixtures

LEFT: The master suite is tucked into a mezza-nine level overlooking the living room. A sliding screen affords privacy.

RIGHT: An intimate garden terrace off the living room was decorated with mosaics by Northwest artist Guy Anderson.

and cabinets Terry created to display the Haubergs' pre-Columbian art collection. Now occupied by Oly and Barbara Wise, the dignified yet daring house retains its singular power after more than forty years. As noted by the writer in *House Beautiful* in 1960, "the many creative skills woven into the fabric of this house give it a depth of personal meaning and contribute to its quality of elegance (or specialness)."

With that statement, the article touched on a quality others have iden-tified in Roland Terry's work. Ralph Anderson, who graduated from the University of Washington several years after Terry, has achieved a substan-tial reputation over forty-seven years of practicing architecture in Seattle. One might safely call him an expert on the Seattle design scene. Of Terry, Anderson says: "He was not involved in a stylized architecture, but was so-phisticated and devoid of fad and style. His work has a timeless quality. This didn't come from the UW training, these were his own ideas. . . . he was

A floor-to-ceiling wall of glass connects the living room with the garden terrace. Double-height ceilings create a sense of spaciousness.

steadfast in his interpretations, and he brought his own concepts and feelings into his work. He really brought himself into his places. He added a bit of soul into his work. His architecture reflected his own feelings and intuitions. Not many architects can do that." Today, architectural students from the University of Washington still visit the Hauberg house, for it has become an icon of Northwest Modernism.

The Blethen House

A FEW YEARS AFTER HE DESIGNED the Hauberg town house Terry created a house for the William K. Blethen family that takes a decidedly different approach, yet manages to achieve an equally striking elegance and originality. An article on this house was published in the same issue of *House Beautiful* in which the Hauberg town house article appeared, thus offering readers a chance to compare two distinctly different Roland Terry projects.

In this instance, the client presented Terry and his collaborator, interior designer Allen Vance Salsbury, with a different kind of challenge. On one hand, hiring an architect like Roland Terry implies the desire for an architect with vision. On the other hand, along with their fundamental programmatic requirements, the Blethens had a rather eccentric wish list, for they asked that the home include multiple balconies, elements reminiscent of Pompeiian villas, and the ambience of an antebellum mansion of the Old South. In addition they had a collection of eighteenth-century furniture to fit seamlessly into the house. This could have been a classic recipe for disaster or at best a disordered pastiche had the architect's vision run head-on with the client's expensive multicultural fantasies and fine antique furniture.

Instead, as noted in *House Beautiful,* Terry and his associates picked up the common thread in the disparate times and places outlined by the Blethens—that common thread being elegance, pure and simple—and reinterpreted it in a contemporary mode, making subtle reference to Pompeii and the Old South without self-consciousness or superficiality: "Strictly speaking, the house is neither Pompeiian nor antebellum. The forms of neither are imitated in it. But it does contain many of the qualities of both."

Integrating stylistic elements from Pompeiian villas and antebellum mansions, Terry still managed a contemporary look in this Lake Washington–area home for the Blethen family.

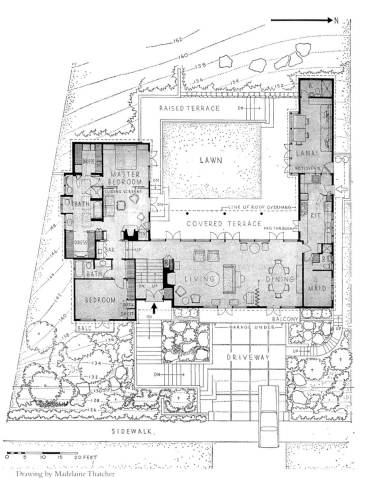

N

162
160
158
156 154 152

RAISED TERRACE   DN

LAWN

LANAI
ROTISSERIE

MASTER
BEDROOM
DRESS
SLIDING SCREENS
DN

BATH

LINE OF ROOF OVERHANG
KIT.

DRESS

COVERED TERRACE
PASS THROUGH

BAR   UP
BATH

LIVING   DINING   MAID
BEDROOM
DRESS
CHEST
DN

BALC   BALCONY

GARAGE UNDER   UP

136
134
132
130
128
126

DRIVEWAY   DN   UP

SIDEWALK.

0 5 10 15 20 FEET

Drawing by Madelaine Thatcher

Plan and photographs show how the U-shaped house wraps around a central courtyard, evoking a Pompeiian villa. Columns and high-ceilinged, grandly scaled volumes subtly recall the Southern manse.

These qualities include stucco as the primary material (an unusual choice in the Northwest at that time), high ceilings, floor-to-ceiling columns, and covered balconies and terraces. The floorplan, which wraps the house in an asymmetrical U-shape around a central courtyard, evokes a Pompeiian villa. Glass walls with sliding doors link living spaces to sheltered terraces that ring the central courtyard on three sides, while a retaining wall—the house and grounds are partly cut into the hillside—provides the fourth "wall" of the courtyard. Black-and-white photographs from 1960 illustrate Terry's ability to create grandly scaled spaces made invitingly intimate through the application of fine finishes and luxurious yet understated details. His mastery of proportion and color made these warmly lit, contemporary spaces perfectly appropriate for the client's antique furniture.

The Pompeiian or antebellum elements Terry subtly evokes with this elegant design bring to mind a quality in his work best described by interior designer Carol Bain, who worked for and with the architect for many years. As Bain put it when discussing Terry's interior design skills: "Roland took the time to acquaint himself with architectural history, edit it down to what was classic, and bring it into the contemporary. He has a masterful mind with a great sense of history, and he has the ability to bring it forward." The "edit it down" part is important here: At the Blethen house, Terry was happy to accommodate the client's request for Pompeiian-style columns, but as he recently noted, "I refused to put the curlicues . . . [requested by Mrs. Blethen] . . . on the columns." Those missing curlicues make a world of difference.

The Jarvis House

AT ABOUT THE SAME TIME HE WAS WORKING on the Blethen house, Terry designed a completely different kind of house for Dr. and Mrs. Jarvis and their children. As an article published in *House Beautiful* in August 1958 illustrates, the Lake Washington waterfront home features practical, child-proof materials, like red brick and raw wood, counterpointed with custom-designed light fixtures and integrated artworks (specifically requested by the client), including a striking mural by Kenneth Callahan on an entry wall by the front door. Approached via a path through a small, elegant Asian-style garden, the oxidized-copper front door is a work of art in itself. Terry exploited the evocative marine green of patinated copper decades before it became a design cliché in the 1980s.

The surprisingly compact but spacious-feeling living room, dining room, and kitchen all flow together, unhindered by walls (sliding translucent screens provide privacy when needed). The architect used natural woods, peeled raw logs (an evolving Terry trademark), and glass walls and doors as counter-points to the primary material, red brick. Brick is an ultimately practical material for floors and even some interior walls: the warm red is inviting, while the material itself is easy to maintain and long-lived. (Current resident Jennifer Naimy recalls hearing that in summertime, once a day the Jarvises would take all the furniture out of these main rooms and wash them down with a hose.) With peeled logs supporting the beams of the peaked ceiling, the lakeside exterior walls are nonstructural, so Terry made them glass, which permits an unobstructed view and flow between the house, the deck, and the lake. Extending the brick floors onto the lakefront terrace and down to the lake, the architect further enhanced the inside-outside connection.

Longtime Terry collaborator Irene McGowan designed the light fixtures for the Jarvis house on Lake Washington.

OPPOSITE: A mural by Kenneth Callahan adorns the entry.

49

Dearborn-Massar

The brick terrace shown here flows inside to form the interior floor as well. The log columns support the roof structure, permitting the installation of a seamless glass wall, which furthers the link between inside and outside.

The plan at right illustrates Terry's practical response to the needs of a large, active family, with the kitchen at the heart of the house, and the public rooms having free access to the outside. By isolating the master suite at one end, Terry gave the parents a measure of privacy, and by extending the glass walls partially across the front of the master bedroom he allowed them to still share in the house's intimate relationship with the waterfront. By putting the children's rooms at the other end of the house, in a single wing with its own heating system, Terry provided the owners the option of shutting down that wing when the children grew up and moved out, and then reactivating it as necessary.

One only need visit the house today to appreciate the success of the project as well as the durability of the brick—for every last brick is still in place. The lake-embracing home, with some small remodels accomplished over the years, remains as inviting today as when it was built some thirty-five years ago. Jennifer Naimy, of the Raphael-Naimy family, who now occupy the house, supports the home's enduring comfort: "We feel blessed that we are able to live in this house. We've never felt we had to change it, we like it as it is."

TOP: The house is open from end to end on the water side. As is evident in the plan, the brick terrace extends via steps directly into the lake.

BOTTOM: Plan shows how the kitchen has been positioned at the pivot point of the house—an innovation precursing the increasingly important role of the kitchen in the modern family home.

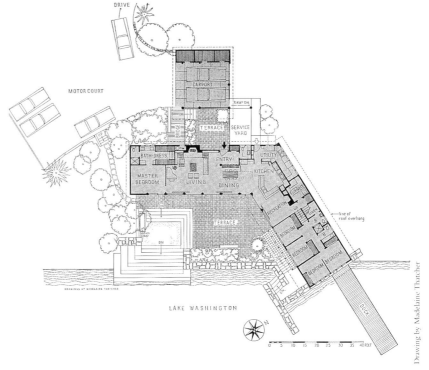

The Day House

DURING THE LATE 1950S TERRY & MOORE designed a number of houses outside Seattle, including a magnificent country house for the John S. Day family on a three-thousand-acre ranch in Central Point, Oregon. The extraordinary wilderness setting, on a hilltop overlooking the Rogue River Valley, allowed Terry to employ his urbane, sophisticated architectural approach in a rural Western context. The results affirm his unique talents: without stinting on his usual refinements and details, Terry created a rambling, rugged structure perfectly suited to the needs of the owners and the wild beauty of the site. Crafted of stone, cedar, and great sweeps of view-making glass, the house's three generously proportioned wings leave an impression of strength, solidity, and epic scale appropriate to the vastness of the wide-open terrain. This is a home made to order for a man with big dreams and big ideas, who owned the land practically as far as the eye could see.

Aesthetics, practicality, and site sensitivity all played a role in the design. The plan on page 54 illustrates a savvy distribution of space, with one wing functioning as a service and dining wing, a second as a master bedroom and office wing (with an apartment underneath), and the third as a living and guest-room wing, linked to the rest of the house by a gallery. Small sets of steps enhance the division of the wings, leading down from the entrance level to the living area and up to the master-bedroom level. The plan shows how the house shelters the pool on two sides. Stone stairs spill from the gallery down to the pool, surrounded by a wide terrace accessible from the master-bedroom and living-room wings.

The interiors reflect the owners' informal style. Slate slab flooring brings the outside in and offers easy maintenance. An overscale stone fireplace—"big

Terry's skillful use of rough materials in refined ways is elegantly demonstrated in the Day house in Oregon, where raw logs form a trellis over an outdoor room and rough stone floors flow from the outside in.

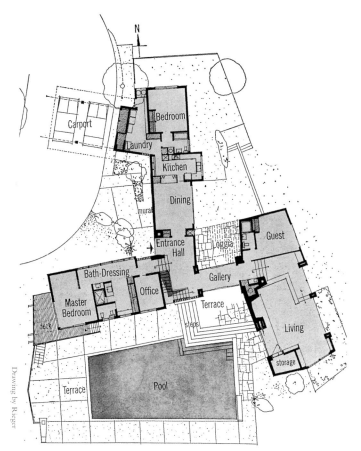

Drawing by Rieger

Dearborn-Massar

LEFT: Plan illustrates the grandly scaled, rambling nature of the house and also demonstrates a brilliant sense of circulation and organization.

RIGHT: The den exhibits trophy heads, stone walls and floors, and other masculine elements, but the furnishings and custom carpet refine the space.

enough to hold six-foot logs," Terry remembers—dominates the denlike living room, which features pine paneling, heavy beams, and wall-mounted hunting trophies, classic elements of the Western ranch-house tradition. Terry then refined this masculine tradition with comfortable, fabric-finished sofas and chairs, custom lighting fixtures, and a woven rug with animal designs. The animals in the rug recall the animals mounted on the wall; they also echo an entry-area fresco of animals and horsemen by Seattle artist Jean Beall, done in a style suggestive of Cro-Magnon cave art. Living room window walls frame dramatic views, while media equipment is efficiently built into walls and cabinets used as room dividers. The dining room strikes a more formal note, with a Japanese mural of cranes counterpointed by a glass wall offering panoramic views of the valley.

Like the Japanese mural in the dining room, the collection of delicate fans mounted in a case over the bed in the master bedroom reflects the more sophisticated side of the Day family. Roland Terry's design effortlessly integrates this aspect with the other elements that comprise the family's eclectic, individualistic style. According to an article in the April 1958 issue of *House & Garden,* the Days consulted twenty-five architectural firms and several

architectural professors before choosing Terry, and Terry worked up five sets of plans before construction began. In the end, as noted in *House & Garden*, "They got the house they wanted, a striking stone and cedar structure that fits the setting admirably. But more important, it fits the needs and satisfies the aspirations of the family living in it."

Rough stone embedded in the deck and stairs gives an Asian cast to this rugged house. The balance of intimacy and grandeur captured here perfectly suited both the client and the site.

The Culter House

CREATING A HOUSE WITH INSPIRED VIEWS and a dynamic interior-exterior relationship becomes a different kind of challenge when the site moves from the wide-open spaces of a rural ranch to a small lot in the suburbs. Roland Terry's design for the Lawrence Culter family home in Vancouver, British Columbia, offers another example of his ability to adapt to the demands of changing sites, making the best use of available space. At first glance, the Culter house has the look of a well-crafted, contemporary suburban home, with a subtle grace that elevates it into a more distinctive realm. However, as is true with most of Terry's buildings, there is more to this house than meets the eye.

Working on a half-acre lot hemmed in on three sides by neighboring houses, Terry created a structure with a compelling set of views and a vibrant interplay of interior and exterior. Or, as the story about the project was rather prosaically titled in the October 1961 issue of *House & Garden*, "How to have a view wherever you look."

Terry sets the stage with his floorplan, which takes into account every square foot of the 150-by-105-foot site, treating both interiors and exteriors as components of the plan. The 3,600-square-foot house, a one-story rambler divided into three levels by short series of steps, spreads out in four directions, forming outdoor "rooms" connected to adjacent interiors via glass walls. Each part of the house is graced with its own exterior space, from which it is virtually inseparable. And at the heart of the property is the courtyard, enclosed on three sides by the house itself and on the fourth by a vine-covered wall. Glass walls and sliding doors provide views and access from all the main rooms into this sunny, sheltered garden.

Skylights flood the kitchen of the Culter house with natural light.

OPPOSITE: The linearity of the 75-foot-long living-dining room is emphasized by the deep lines of the ceiling's reed paneling.

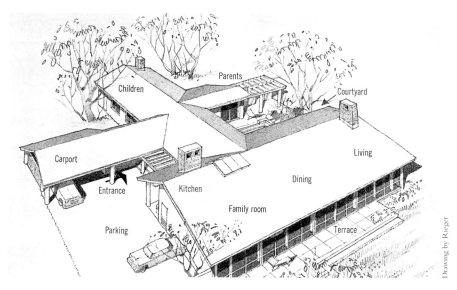

LEFT: A sheltered entry features the same reed-paneled ceiling as the living room, enhancing inside-outside continuity.

RIGHT AND OPPOSITE: Drawing and photo show the intimate relationship of the home's interior rooms with adjacent exterior courtyard gardens.

The home's interiors artfully balance rugged, outdoors-inspired materials with more elegant, luxurious finishes, an interplay that enhances the rich connection of the interiors with the gardens, courtyards, and views. In the living room, peeled cedar-log columns and rough-sawn beams contrast with the finely finished reed-panel ceiling, the teak cabinetry and bar doors, and the ebony bar details (these unusual hardwoods were specified at the request of the owners, who operated a hardwood factory). The dramatic scale of the 50-foot-long room—75 feet including the partially separated family room—is emphasized by the row of cedar columns and the long, deep lines of the ceiling grooves. With the beams supporting the roof structure, window walls float free, while sliding glass doors link the living-room interior with an adjacent terrace. This grandly scaled indoor-outdoor room, counterpointed by the solid wall on the living room's other side, demonstrates a fine-tuned interplay of transparency and opacity.

As is evident in the drawings and photographs, the house rambles without losing coherence or a sense of warmth and comfort. The design balances the grandeur of the high-ceilinged, open-plan living wing with human-scale pleasures: furniture grouped around the hearth and other gathering places, the quiet beauty of the inner courtyard, the informal pleasure of dining at a trestle table.

Terry's design creates an aura of comfort and well-being through artful materials and furnishings, meticulous attention to every detail, sensitivity to the subtle uses of light, and a remarkable instinct for right proportions. And then, in the midst of all that ease of proportion, he strikes a dramatic note with a splash of unexpected color, an indoor water feature, or a volume so generously expansive as to take the breath away.

The Hauberg Country House

TERRY'S UNERRING SENSE OF PROPORTION emerges with rough elegance in his design for the Hauberg country house on Bainbridge Island. Created in the late 1950s as a retreat for John and Anne Gould Hauberg, the house presents a one-story alternative to the multilevel town house Terry designed for them a few years earlier. Whereas Anne Gould Hauberg masterminded the town house, John Hauberg worked with Terry on the design of the Bainbridge Island waterfront project.

Originally built for use as a summer house only, the Bainbridge Island home represents an effort to achieve what John Hauberg describes as "European flavor mixed with Northwest influences." As Hauberg recalls it, he and Terry drove around the island looking at other houses he liked, then Terry worked up an H-shaped plan. Essentially, Hauberg asked for a completely open building with relatively deep overhangs for protection from the weather: a glass house with a good roof. Although a decade-later renovation made the house more weatherproof, the virtual transparency of the structure remains evident in photographs dating from the early 1980s, after the renovation. Terry's signature peeled logs, expansive glass walls, and rugged stonework are all visible. The marriage of house and site is flawless, with stone floors seamlessly connecting the interiors and exteriors, and counterpointing the glass walls.

John Hauberg unabashedly admires Roland Terry. "I think he has a terrific vision," he says, "and tremendous good taste. His rooms were always just right in size and shape, with great circulation and windows. There's no question about his talent. He ranks with Neutra and the others of that generation. I think he was the outstanding architect of his day for residences."

In Terry's hands, tough materials make elegant forms, and doors, like this one on the Hauberg country house, become works of art.

OPPOSITE: The Hauberg country house: essentially a glass box with a big roof. Inside and outside are one, while the roof shelters both.

Photo: © 1980 Dick Busher

61

ABOVE AND OPPOSITE: Stone floors and wood beams provide the grounding elements, while glass walls, skylights, plentiful greenery, and colorful artwork create a rich, inviting atmosphere.

COMMERCIAL WORK

DURING THE 1950S TERRY & MOORE also completed a range of commercial projects, primarily restaurants but also some retail stores and offices. Commercial architecture and design generally have a shorter lifespan than residential, and so over the past forty years many of these projects have been remodeled or replaced by other buildings or with other interiors serving different purposes. Fortunately, many of the projects were photographed and/or published in various design magazines, and so a rich visual and contemporaneous written record remains. While perusing these buildings and interiors, bear in mind that these projects were completed in the now-distant past of the 1950s and early 1960s. In many instances, Terry & Moore broke new conceptual ground for that era.

Canlis Broiler, Waikiki Beach

SURELY ONE OF THE MOST STRIKING restaurant designs of the 1950s, the Canlis Broiler on Waikiki Beach, in Hawaii, was described by its owner as "the most beautiful restaurant in the world," according to *Interiors Magazine,* which published an article on the restaurant in May 1956. A collaborative effort by Terry & Moore with Wimberly & Cook, A.I.A., of Honolulu, the restaurant offers an artful integration of richly elaborated Polynesian and Hawaiian motifs in a clean, elegant modern design. The high-beamed ceiling and copper roof evoke Pacific island structures. Coupled with the rugged stone columns and heavy beams of the interior, these elements establish a solid architectural grounding. The floorplan provides a clear, functional organization of space that permitted the designers to lavish their imaginative efforts on the interior finishes and landscapes.

The Terry & Moore design team collaborated with Ben Norris, chairman of the University of Hawaii's Art Department, on the artwork, colors, and plantings for the 6,000-square-foot interior. Terry took advantage of the balmy Hawaiian climate to explore and exploit even more deeply one of his favored devices—the integration of landscape into architecture and interior. Here, a wall of ferns and orchids and an indoor garden establish a verdant, tropical ambience within the restaurant. The exotic mood created by the lush plantings is deepened by the addition of thematically appropriate artwork: a 14-foot carved wood Polynesian god, a lava-rock mosaic wall, and both vertical and horizontal "fish ponds," populated with multicolored ceramic fish.

In recent years tourists and travelers have been overexposed to thematic restaurants. In the 1950s, however, the Canlis Broiler's respectful and

Canlis Broiler, Waikiki Beach, was one of the first restaurants to employ Polynesian motifs in a tasteful way to attract tourists.

R. Wenkam

sophisticated celebration of Hawaiian culture, designed to appeal to mainland tourists visiting Honolulu, represented an innovative approach to marketing a Hawaiian dining experience. At the Canlis Broiler, Terry and his associates broke new ground, balancing the exotic appeal of Hawaiian and Polynesian motifs with a modern sense of elegance and restraint.

Panels and upholstery enhance the Polynesian theme of the interior. At the time of opening the owner proudly called the Canlis Broiler, "the most beautiful restaurant in the world."

OPPOSITE: Ceramic fish swim up an interior fountain surrounded by a wall of lush tropical vegetation including ferns and orchids.
Photo: R. Wenkam

The Windjammer Restaurant

LOCATED AT SHILSHOLE MARINA in Seattle's Ballard neighborhood, the Windjammer represented an effort by Terry to create a restaurant around the theme of Northwest marine and boating life, ranging from past to present. The historic seafaring roots of the region are first evoked in the entryway, where a portrait of Peter Puget, explorer and namesake of Puget Sound, dominates a colorful wall mural by James Wegner. Throughout the interior, forms and finishes employ oceanic motifs and Puget Sound's lively history. Ship models, captain's chairs, heavy wood beams, wood paneling, globes, myriad nautical objects, and saillike window treatments enhance the effect. Glass walls opening onto a deck that overlooks the boat-filled marina establish the ultimate connection to the boating life, again demonstrating Terry's commitment to integrating his designs with the environment of the site.

Located at Seattle's Shilshole Marina, the Windjammer employed the nautical history of the Northwest as its theme. Captain's chairs and seafaring decorative objects enrich the shipboard effect. Photos: Chas. R. Pearson

The Crabapple and Other Walter Clark Restaurants

BEGINNING WITH CLARK'S CRABAPPLE in 1954, Terry & Moore designed several restaurants for Walter Clark, one of Seattle's most prominent restaurateurs. These projects, including the Red Carpet, in downtown Seattle, and the Bellevue Terrace Dining Room, near Tacoma, established the firm's reputation for innovative, successful commercial work. Terry rather modestly describes his thinking about restaurant design: "Doing restaurants was always fun. I always felt the most important thing was to make sure people were comfortable."

From that simple concept flowed a number of original designs, each dictated by the specific circumstances of the project. The Crabapple, in Bellevue, was one of Terry's first designs for Clark, and like the Seattle Canlis, it incorporated natural Northwest materials in its interiors. Unlike Canlis, however, the Crabapple had served as a casual, drop-in kind of neighborhood place and although the owners were seeking to re-create it as a destination dining room, they did not want to lose the connection with the neighborhood. To this end, Terry established an informal mood with an open-top broiler in the dining room and a pair of fireplaces—one in the vestibule made of local sandstone and a second in the bar made of used brick. Brick and dark-stained spruce walls warm the dining room, while rough-sawn, dark-stained Douglas fir beams and bleached red cedar support posts enhance the regional mood. Specially commissioned artwork and bright upholstery colors stand out against these earthy, unpretentious materials. As is typical of Terry's restaurant work, the seamless integration of colors, textures, materials, and furnishings results in an interior that perfectly balances casual comfort and elegant style.

Simple and informal, yet stylish, the Crabapple featured groundbreaking interiors for its time and illustrates Terry's dictum that in restaurants "the most important thing is to make sure people are comfortable."

71

Terry was the consummate commercial interior designer: the
Red Carpet in downtown Seattle featured a custom-designed
wine rack and a striking mural, a collage of menus.

At the Red Carpet in downtown Seattle, the designers transformed a fast-food coffee shop into an elegant dining room meant to entice patrons with more time and money on their hands than the previous clientèle. White tablecloths and chandeliers established the refined ambience, while brick walls, custom-designed wine racks, and a collage of graphically striking menu designs added visual and textural richness. Terry's intention—to make diners comfortable—was realized, but there was more to the Red Carpet than comfort. In its time, this was a compelling and original space, one of the first urbane dining rooms at a time when Seattle's downtown had little in the way of sophistication.

At the Bellevue Terrace Dining Room, near Tacoma, the intent was to create a space sympathetic to the predominantly colonial-style architecture of the suburban shopping center where the restaurant was located. However, Terry's take on "colonial" style veers from the norm: interior walls are clad with aged wood, suggesting the past, but the red carpeting and furniture have a more contemporary cast. With these touches of refinement, Terry brought a measure of elegance to an essentially provincial outpost.

For the Bellevue Terrace Dining Room, located near Tacoma in a colonial-themed shopping center, Terry evoked the past with aged wood, then turned it upscale a notch with red carpeting and custom light fixtures and furnishings.

The Dublin House Restaurant

ONE OF THE MOST POPULAR TERRY & MOORE restaurants of the late 1950s and early 1960s was the Dublin House, commissioned by Walter Clark for a ground-floor location in a downtown Seattle office building. Prior to fitting out the Dublin House, Terry and Clark took a ten-day whirlwind trip to Ireland in search of accessories. As Terry remembers it, they bought the entire contents of at least one Irish pub, and much of it ended up on the walls of this restaurant. Even English visitors were impressed—Terry recalls being told by visitors that he had done a better job of re-creating a Georgian club-style restaurant than the English did in London.

In England and Ireland, such restaurant interiors might develop organically, with decorative touches and accessories accruing over a period of decades, even centuries. The Dublin House, on the other hand, was assembled in a matter of weeks. What is striking about the interior, experienced in retrospect via photographs, is the lack of thematic clutter. While most of the accessories came with the patina and pedigree of aged objects, Terry also bought a couple of contemporary Irish paintings, which found their way into the design as well. Often, in artificially assembled "period" dining rooms, what passes as coziness when developed organically comes off as stuffiness when the atmosphere is forcibly sentimentalized, but there is none of that here. The Dublin House is steeped in authentic Irish Georgian style, and yet its serene elegance has as much to do with the organization of space and the meticulous placement of objects as it does with the emotional or artistic value inherent in the imported objects themselves. As Terry put it, "We had a lot of very good stuff in there, and it was organized in a very careful way." His ability to embrace fully the elements of thematic design

Dearborn-Massar

In its heyday, the Dublin House, in downtown Seattle, was the city's most sophisticated dining room, all decked out with accessories purchased by Terry on a whirlwind trip to Ireland.

RIGHT AND OPPOSITE: Elegantly crowded with artwork purchased in Ireland, the rich wood paneling of the Dublin House conjured the charm of Georgian-style clubs.

without being overwhelmed by them is another mark of his originality: the more common fate of themed restaurants is total overkill, with the visual volume turned up so loud the rest is drowned out. From the evidence in other photographs of the Dublin House, the Windjammer, and other themed rooms, this was never a problem in Roland Terry restaurants.

Cristiana Restaurant

FOR THE CRISTIANA RESTAURANT in Ketchum, Idaho, Terry designed a Bavarian A-frame style structure, appropriate to the mountainous ski country of Sun Valley. Spanned with rugged beams, the open-ceilinged A-frame creates a dramatically oversized environment for the main dining room. A terrace off this spacious volume establishes a patio for al fresco summer dining. The bar and lounge occupy the second level, several steps up from the dining room, while a mezzanine level provides space for private dining.

Regional materials tie this "Bavarian" building to its Idaho location. The interior walls are paneled with weathered silver-gray siding from local barns, while the stone walls are constructed of a bluish tinged local stone naturally layered with the organic colors of lichen. Cork ceilings and plaid banquette finishes complement the polished roughness of the regionalist approach, as do the custom lighting fixtures designed by the architects in collaboration with industrial designer Irene McGowan.

Stone and weathered siding from local barns link the Bavarian-style Cristiana Restaurant to its mountain location in Idaho.
Photos: Dearborn-Massar

Japan Air Lines Office

TERRY & MOORE'S LATE 1950S AND EARLY 1960S work also included several retail and office projects, notably a spare, Asian-influenced office for Japan Air Lines. Years before the minimalist ethos of the Japanese aesthetic had taken hold in American design circles, Roland Terry employed it here. Located in a long, narrow space in downtown Seattle, the Japan Air Lines office demonstrates Terry's affinity for Asian design at its best, while affirming his skill at space planning to great functional effect.

Terry placed the manager's office at the rear and used sliding screens to cut it off from the more public areas. Other screens, along with decorative "obi" panels and recessed areas—for seating or art display—divide the space into smaller sections, countering the tunnellike shape of the office. To uphold the almost zenlike simplicity of the interior, storage units behind sliding, grass cloth–covered panels along both walls contain print matter that would otherwise clutter the space. Dark woods with contrasting light-toned panels contribute to the Japanese ambience; the same contrast works with the dark desks set against the light-colored floor. A Japanese symbol on the front door is repeated on the floor, helping to unify the design. Again, Terry has employed powerful ethnic imagery to create a mood and to enhance a commercial message. He has done so without overdoing the motifs, while demonstrating understanding and respect for the culture whose design sensibility served as source and inspiration.

Terry was one of the first American designers to explore the potential for austere elegance in Japan's minimalist style—perfectly appropriate for the Japan Air Lines office in Seattle.

Crissey Florist

THE CRISSEY FLORIST SHOP IN SEATTLE counterpoints the verdant appeal of potted plants—an urban version of the natural Northwest world that inspires so many of Roland Terry's designs—with lively graphic and decorative elements appropriate to a city shop selling flowers and plants. A harlequin-patterned door makes for an eye-catching entry, which flanked by glass walls transforms the entire shop into a glowing lantern, a brilliantly lit greenhouse visible from the street. Inside, black and white tiles create a powerful graphic rhythm on the floor, while brick walls make a warming backdrop. Metal decorative elements such as door handles as well as display tables and shelves feature floral and leaf forms and enhance the organic, plant-inspired quality of the interior with a sophisticated flourish. Skillfully working within the parameters of the program, Terry here employs motifs that reinforce the products for sale without overwhelming them.

At Crissey Florist, Terry added graphic punch to a simple, glass-walled storefront by using a harlequin pattern in the doors and entry.

Photos: Dearborn-Massar

Part III

THE MASTER AT WORK

1960 THROUGH 1990

BY 1960, WHEN THE TERRY & MOORE partnership dissolved and Roland Terry took on the role of sole principal of Roland Terry AIA and Associates, he was established as one of the Seattle area's most highly regarded residential and commercial architects. Over the next several decades, until retiring in the early 1990s, Terry designed and built dozens of architecturally outstanding residences and numerous restaurants, hotels, offices, and other commercial projects. Although the firm changed its name, grew, and evolved, Terry's architectural skill remained a constant—the creative force that drove the business.

Fortunately for those architectural aficionados among us who were not around when Terry was working, most of his residential clients and a few commercial clients as well, have seen fit to leave his architecture alone for the most part. This, despite changing lifestyles and tastes in interior finishes and furnishings, which have led to renovations and remodels of varying degree. However, in the residential arena, even those projects that have been extensively remodeled often appear untouched or minimally altered. Many of the architects commissioned for these remodels have been great admirers of Terry's work, so they did all they could to preserve the original architecture while accommodating the needs of the home owners. We are thus able to use recent photographs to illustrate several houses in this section that were designed and built in the 1960s. Likewise, in spite of renovations, many hotels that Terry designed in the 1960s remain true to the spirit of the original design.

Before embarking on our project-by-project exploration of Roland Terry's peak years as an architect, some point/counterpoint may be useful.

OPPOSITE: An eclectic assortment of books, artwork, and interesting objects and finishes from the house Terry designed for himself on Lopez Island (see pp. 110–15) illustrates his sense of worldly, cultivated style. Photo: © John Vaughan, Photographer. © 2000 The Condé Nast Publications Inc. All rights reserved. Used with permission.

One cannot research the career of an architect working at the level of Roland Terry without running into some controversy. Terry has detractors: disgruntled former partners, disappointed clients, others not enamored of every building he has done. For example, the Washington Park Tower on the shore of Lake Washington had its critics, who complained about the building's view-blocking mass and overwhelming vertical presence on the flat, horizontal lakeside. In an article titled "Master of Costly Design," which appeared in the June 1967 issue of *Seattle Magazine,* Terry presented his own defense of the building: "Soon nobody's going to be able to afford a single-family residence on the water that close to town . . . what has to come is tall, slender towers that permit plenty of parkland and view."

Some contend that the design for the original Seattle Canlis should have been attributed as much to partners Tucker and Shields as to Roland Terry, since evidence suggests Terry was not around during the design process—he was in Europe when the project was on the boards. However, the argument does not stand up when you learn that Peter Canlis subsequently hired Terry to design Canlis restaurants in Waikiki Beach, Portland, and San Francisco (see pp. 64–67 and 152–53).

Over the years others have noted that Terry often found it difficult to hold the line on a budget. However, like any architect intent on doing good work, Terry didn't want to limit the possibilities for a project. If his designs called for the most expensive materials or applications—particularly when he knew the clients could afford the extra cost—he wouldn't hesitate to specify them. In the same vein, another "problem" was Terry's penchant for endlessly reworking details and even major elements in a design, leading to delays and budget overruns. However, as Thomas Veith pointed out in *Shaping Seattle Architecture,* "It was this constant refinement of detail and the integration of other visual arts that gave Terry's work its unique character."[1]

Robert Egan, associate and partner, noted Terry's inability to get along with "business types." He claims one reason Terry made him a partner was his talent for dealing with the bottom line—and the bottom-line bean-counters who ran the hotel companies whose business they were after in the 1960s and 1970s. Egan adds: "Roland had difficulties dealing with clients at times, because he wasn't always practical, and he didn't always explain what he was doing." And yet Terry was smart enough to bring Egan along to handle the clients.

Whatever problems Terry may have engendered with his idiosyncratic approach to running a business, he managed to get dozens of exceptional projects designed and most of them built. He left a legacy of distinct and memorable buildings, many of which are still occupied today.

1. Jeffrey Karl Ochsner, ed., *Shaping Seattle Architecture: A Historical Guide to the Architects* (Seattle: University of Washington Press, 1994), p. 273.

Allen Vance Salsbury worked with Terry on different projects over a period of decades and lived in a house Terry originally designed for Paul Roland Smith (see pp. 96–99) for a number of years. He is an admirer of Terry's work and a lifelong friend as well. "He was very inspiring," Salsbury says. "He presented his ideas forcefully but in a kind way. He was wonderful to work with. There were never arguments because he was positive, persuasive, and diplomatic. His designs always had elegance, for he took the raw materials of the Northwest and presented them in a refined way. He has great style, and I admire his work a great deal."

Terry's cousin Laura Ingham puts it another way: "He educates you so that you understand why he has designed something the way he has, and after you understand it, it is so obvious that you'd never want to do it another way. He might say, 'When you eat breakfast, you want to enjoy the light of early morning, don't you? Then you need a window on the east side!'"

A chorus of former employees and associates offered their views of how Terry's office worked and how Roland operated. According to Michael Cunningham, who worked for Terry through much of the 1970s' Terry & Egan period,

> Every single job was completely different. Roland would do interiors if people wanted them done, because he could design anything and everything. He would meet with clients, go to the site, then make his decisions. He always ran the show. He would do watercolors and drawings, and then the plan would develop. He worked without limits, using rough materials in sophisticated ways. His interiors were always dramatic, but never at the expense of being livable. He usually got his way with clients, but at the same time they were always happy. I think he was an important guy because he's an original—he can't be copied, and unlike most architects, he did everything well. It is important to note that his interiors did not undermine the spaces that he had created. When he designed the building, he designed the insides as well; and he always tied the building to the site.

Mark Daniels worked for Roland Terry and Associates from 1979 through the 1980s and helped Terry complete some of the later projects in his career, including the Halekulani Hotel in Honolulu (see pp. 146–49) —recently judged the number one hotel in the world by the readers of *Gourmet Magazine*—and the Stevenson residence in the Columbia River Gorge. He says simply that "Roland was extremely gifted as a designer. He was very subtle and paid great attention to detail and proportion. He was never flamboyant but designed little jewel boxes—or big jewel boxes, as

PROPOSED RESIDENCE for MR. and MRS. CHARLES W. LOOMIS
on WEBSTER POINT · LAURELHURST · SEATTLE   JUNE 29, 1966
ROLAND TERRY A.I.A. & ASSOCIATES · ARCHITECTS · SEATTLE

A PROPOSED RESIDENCE in the "HIGHLANDS" for MR. & MRS. SPENCER CLARK
TERRY & MOORE · ARCHITECTS · INTERIOR DESIGN · SEATTLE · WN.   NOV. 15, 1960

the case may be. Anyone that worked with Roland—once the rapport was established and he had confidence in that person—worked as an extension of him. He would do very detailed sketches and then hand them off to get the drawings done. These sketches were almost always scalable; you could put a scale to one and it would work. This was impressive because it was both artistic and practical."

Robert Egan began working for Roland Terry as a draftsman in the 1960s and was promoted to associate and eventually to partner. Egan remains a fan of Terry and his work.

> Roland was a very good designer, and I learned one heck of a lot from him. He always had this great philosophy. I was taught that as an architect, you shouldn't be planning interiors or specifying fabric or doing any of the things that interior designers do, but Roland taught me that you don't just do the outside of the building, you do the whole thing. Whether it's a store, a house, a hotel, or a restaurant, you do the total package, because everything relates to everything else.

> Roland was a responsive boss, and very fair. He took me under his wing, and I listened to and grew with him. I'll always credit him for a lot of my direction. He was an excellent architect because he did not believe in doing something new just to be new. That was not his approach, because he believed it was a disservice to the public.

> When we were doing restaurants his foremost idea was to make people comfortable. This is not accomplished by constantly changing things and chasing after trends. Instead, you stay within the existing concept, so it will last. We did not do Hollywood stuff with a new look every three years. This was true for his houses as well. They were always designed with proportion in mind, and how it felt to move from room to room. The first image upon entry—what you see—was important, and every space or room had its importance in relation to the others.

> A lot of people said Roland's designs cost too much money, which was often true, due to the level of detailing. The houses were always richly detailed, to the point where the details didn't stand out individually but instead formed a whole. This meant that people would enter a room and like it, without immediately focusing on a single element. The designs encompassed everything, and everything knit together. Yet the houses were totally different, each possessing its own character.

OPPOSITE: In the design phase, Terry usually completed elaborately detailed drawings and watercolors, and the end product generally emerged looking very much like the drawings.

At the Philip and Marvell Stewart house (see pp. 100–105), Terry created a sheltered exterior colonnade (foreground) and a teahouse (center background), linked to the main building via an indoor gallery. Every room offers a view of Puget Sound.

Jim Mayeno began working with Roland Terry at Terry & Moore in 1953 and worked with him for over twenty-five years. Robert Egan called him Roland's "right-hand man." He probably knows Terry's modus operandi as well as anyone:

Roland did the original design on tracing paper, spending hours on it. Then he'd give it to me, and I'd make an architectural drawing. He designed from the outside in and from the inside out. He was always conscious of the interiors and laid out furniture in the preliminary stages. He was very adaptable and well based in classical architectural styles.

Roland was a good listener. He never forced the issues. He took the clients' needs and then worked them through his own visions. He would come up with the design, then sketch it with furniture already laid out. We'd do a hard line drawing and then he'd meet with the clients. He had great design sense, and a great

© 1999 Donna Day

Details often transform the simplest elements. To hold the bases of structural posts in the Stewart residence, Terry created plinths styled after similar ones in a temple in Kyoto, Japan. Alternating black and white steps adds graphic appeal and makes the steps easier to see.

feeling for proportion, and he knew interiors really well, so his places are very livable, with a wonderful sense of color.

These voices from Terry's associates echo and expand on the same design themes voiced by the architects in Part I, a reiteration that serves to underline the consistency of Terry's design philosophy over the long span of his career. Though he created dozens of buildings and never really repeated himself, he always worked with the same attitude: design everything down to the last detail, so that it all fits together, fits into the site, and is comfortable and livable. He shaped the view of the mountain, yet he also chose the color of the stones in the garden and the upholstery in the living room.

The rich originality of his work, imbued with zenlike clarity and a Palladian sense of proportion, earns him a lofty spot in the pantheon of Northwest architects.

RESIDENTIAL WORK

ROLAND TERRY'S STRENGTHS AS A DESIGNER have always arisen, in part, out of his innate talent for building to accommodate the civilized human being, and so it comes as no surprise that many of his greatest projects have been single family residences. After all, the private house is perhaps the most civilized—and civilizing—of all architectural forms. In the privacy of their own homes people find the physical and psychological space to fully and comfortably express themselves. Terry's gift might be described as an ability to help his clients discover how best to do that.

The pages that follow illuminate Terry's residential work from the 1960s through the 1990s, during the most productive and inspired decades of his long, illustrious career. The virtues of these houses, whether new or renovations, remain subtle. While each is possessed of its own singular charms, all offer the pleasures of excellent proportions and exquisite details; and though built to suit the needs of demanding, individualist clients, they remain distinctly recognizable as Terry projects.

803 East Prospect

ALTHOUGH THIS PROJECT REPRESENTS a relatively light renovation rather than new construction, because it served as Terry's home and office for many years, it seemed appropriate to include it in this section of the book. The 803 East Prospect house, found for Terry by his mother, Florence Beach Terry, also reveals his design philosophy from a different angle: here, what he chose not to do is as important as what he did. Or, as *House Beautiful* titled a story on the house in the September 1963 issue: "Maybe drastic changes aren't needed."

Constructed in 1909, the Tudor-style house had devolved from a grand, single-family residence to a slightly shabby boardinghouse over the course of about fifty years. However, beneath the shabbiness lay a real turn-of-the-century gem, a solid, well-constructed house finished with ornate decorative plaster ceilings, carved oak staircases, and rich wood paneling throughout. The driveway offered direct access to the front door's sheltering entrance canopy, and the main garden area lay to the south of the house, sheltered from the street yet positioned to take maximum advantage of the oft-scarce Seattle sun.

More important from Terry's point of view, the house had a well-conceived plan, and the rooms were well proportioned, well situated, and appropriately scaled in relation to each other and to the house as a whole. Roland Terry greatly admires the Italian Neoclassical architect Andrea Palladio, and his home-office at 803 East Prospect seemingly was possessed of the ineffable rightness of scale and proportion that has dignified the work of Palladio and his disciples down through the centuries. And so Terry remodeled the house and gardens and distributed the living quarters, client

Terry lived and worked in this 1909 home on Seattle's Capitol Hill. In the living room, he painted the ceiling white to show off the moldings, while he stripped the white paint off the walls to expose the Western cedar woodwork.

reception, meeting rooms, and office areas throughout the three floors. What stands revealed by the work here is the timelessness of Terry's approach to design: deeply appreciative of the excellent bones of the house, he kept his changes minimal and most were executed to enhance or bring to light qualities inherent in the original architecture.

In the living room, for example, he stripped away multiple coats of white paint to expose the Western red cedar woodwork, and he painted the ceiling white to reestablish the room's proportions and better show off the plaster molding. He replaced boldly patterned Victorian wallpaper with Japanese silk paper, which has a more subtle finish, to set off the room's ornamentation rather than fight it. He had the floor bleached to tone down the color and removed a pair of chandeliers to open up the volume. The chandeliers were then transformed into candelabras, which he placed on tables flanking the fireplace. In total, with a few relatively simple decorative changes Terry transformed the period room into a contemporary space without sacrificing architectural integrity or ornamental richness.

In the dining room Terry also stripped the floor. Here, he installed a rewired eighteenth-century French chandelier and added handmade Belgian

flame lights underneath for added sparkle. Low-voltage spotlights concealed in ceiling coffers highlight artwork. With the conversion of a sunroom into a study and the placement of an eclectic mix of furnishings, the interior renovation was more or less complete.

Terry also transformed the garden; he replaced quadrants of grass formed by paths crossing at a central sundial with a low-maintenance, intensive-use brick patio. A second brick terrace was extended from the west side of the house, establishing another outdoor room for use in the afternoons. Watercourses, carved totems, and Mexican statuary enhance the livability of these diverse outdoor spaces. An architect less sure of himself perhaps would have felt compelled to leave a more lasting mark on this fine old house, but Terry altered with a light, confident hand, respecting the integrity of the existing structure while transforming it into a contemporary home and office.

ABOVE: Well-stocked built-in bookshelves, generous windows, and appealing furnishings make the library-study a warm, welcoming place for meetings or simply relaxing.

OPPOSITE TOP: In the dining room, Terry stripped the floors to the original wood and added a rewired eighteenth-century chandelier.

OPPOSITE BOTTOM: Terry always looked to create intimate spaces—inside and out. His patios and gardens nicely balance the natural and the man-made.

The Paul Roland Smith House

TERRY'S EARLY 1960S DESIGN for the Paul Roland Smith house, near Seattle's Lake Washington, is organized around a centrally located garden atrium sheltered by a high, skylighted roof—a rectangular elevated section with clerestory windows that enhance the flood of light from the translucent ceiling. The inspiration for the design came from a magazine article clients had read about a house configured around a central gathering room. Terry chose to make this room an indoor garden—a "tropical" interior decorated with a fountain and numerous lush, oversize plantings—that would provide a perpetually green, outdoorslike experience in a sheltered interior and permit the owners to entertain in their garden any time they wished, regardless of the rainy Seattle weather. The atrium has much in common with a courtyard: the living areas of the house wrap around it, providing the kind of inside-out intimate garden views Terry favored in many of his houses. Glass walls and sliding glass doors connect the indoor garden and the other interior volumes with the house's real gardens—terraces to the south and west—expanding the sense of space within and underlining the dynamic relationship of interior to exterior.

The house presents an understated yet handsome facade to the street, with a pair of dignified doors signaling the entry. Beyond these doors, a clearly delineated vestibule serves as transition space between the street and the interior and sets the stage for the moment of impact, when the light-bathed, generous volumes of the interior stand revealed. The high atrium ceilings and glass walls expand the sense of interior space, lending this rather compact two-bedroom house the feel of a much larger volume. At one point, previous owner Allen Salsbury says, people wanted to buy the house

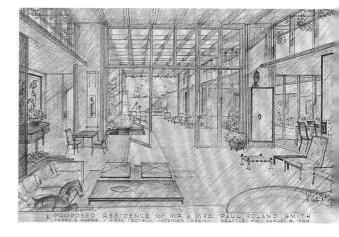

Drawing illuminates the transparent, luminous quality of Terry's original design for the Paul Roland Smith house.

OPPOSITE: The home features a central indoor atrium bathed in light from clerestories and skylights. Photo: © 1999 Donna Day

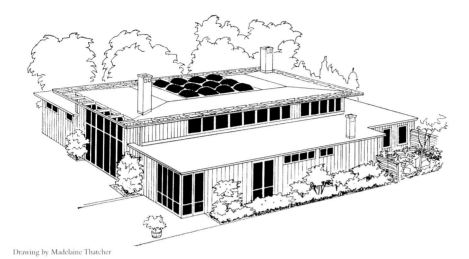

Drawing by Madelaine Thatcher

TOP: Drawing shows clerestories and skylights around the central atrium and also illustrates how the building is organized around that central elevated space. The house has been minimally altered since being designed and built in the early 1960s.

BOTTOM: A small enclosed garden is characterized by an almost Asian sense of spare, austere grace.

and turn it into a reception space for fund-raising parties and other such events. Although neighborhood resistance put an end to that idea, it reflects well on the qualities of spaciousness and harmony that prevail in the house.

More recently, Salsbury commissioned architect George Suyama to make some renovations to the house. Responding to changes in lifestyle that have taken place in recent decades, Suyama opened up the once-isolated kitchen to the dining room and to the street. But since both Suyama and Salsbury greatly admire Terry's work, the house was little changed. The wood and glass interior, set off by the original polished terrazzo floor, remains much the same as Terry designed it—and remains an inviting, beautifully detailed and harmoniously scaled house.

Allen Salsbury sold the house in 1999, and the current owner has hired Jim Olson, of Olson Sundberg, to do another round of renovations. Fortunately, Olson is a big fan of Roland Terry, so it appears fairly certain the house's architectural integrity will be maintained into the foreseeable future.

A long view of the central atrium reveals the sense of generous scale in what is essentially a small house. Glass walls link the gardenlike interior to terraces, left and right.

The Philip & Marvell Stewart House

POSITIONED IN THE NORTH END OF SEATTLE, high on a bluff overlooking Puget Sound, the rambling, two-story Stewart house represents a serendipitous meeting of the minds of client and architect. Philip and Marvell Stewart had spent a fair amount of time in Japan prior to commissioning the house in the early 1960s, and they were great admirers of Japanese homes. Roland Terry's work had always been subtly influenced by Japanese design, for he had long ago recognized that the "Japanese idiom is very modern." While not strictly Japanese, the house Terry created for the Stewarts during a two-year period while they lived and worked in Tokyo, represents a Northwest-influenced distillation of Japanese architecture.

As was noted in an article published in *House & Garden* in November 1966, the Japanese essence of this expansive, view-oriented house lies in its basic construction—with exposed posts and beams supporting sloping peaked roofs. This building method frees the exterior walls from serving as supports, so Terry was able to make them of sliding glass, or, where privacy required, of lightweight but opaque screen material. In classic Terry style, the combination of peaked ceilings and glass walls creates generously scaled interior volumes while establishing a powerful connection between the interior and the natural world outside.

Materials strengthen this connection and also enhance the Japanese influence. Both inside and out, the support posts are set in pewter-colored plinths of cast concrete, designed after similar plinths in a temple in Kyoto. The posts are natural cedar trunks with the bark removed. Without removing the irregularities, the posts and beams were stained a deep walnut and rubbed to a soft shine. "The ceiling beams were all very dark, almost black,"

Bronze hands from Thailand form a gesture of welcome in the Stewart house.

OPPOSITE: Dark-stained posts and beams contrast with a honey-colored peaked ceiling in this house inspired by Japanese design.
Photo: © 1999 Donna Day

Accessed from the house via sliding glass walls, multiple decks, plantings, and stairs connect the house with the swimming pool.

RIGHT: Meticulous, intimate gardens enhance the Asian atmosphere.

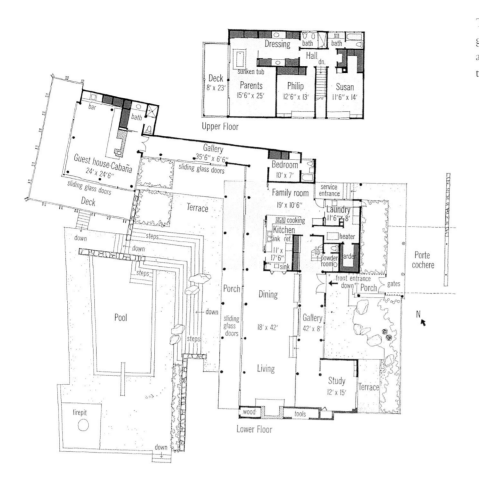

The floor and site plan shows how the house gently embraces the pool. The second story is a compact unit positioned directly over the center of the structure.

notes Terry. "While the areas between were very light, so the ceiling [of honey-stained reeded hemlock] appeared to float atop the beams." Beneath this high ceiling the living room stretches 42 feet from end to end. Enclosed on the west or view side by a wall of sliding glass doors, it opens on the other side to the entrance gallery, a few steps higher. On the entry, or east, side of this gallery, a shorter span of glass opens onto a small Japanese garden, establishing a "dialogue" of intimate garden view and expansive territorial view and lending the living room a wonderfully spacious quality.

As is evident in the plan and photographs, the rambling house is generously scaled but at the same time the design is functionally well executed, with much consideration given to the working relationships between rooms. For example, Terry designed folding doors and multipurpose cabinets to enclose the kitchen yet permit it to be opened to the family room, terrace, and dining area, which lies between the kitchen and the living room. The second story occupies a relatively small area directly over the kitchen and

family room; with the master suite and children's bedrooms upstairs, this compact zone comprises the whole of the two-story core of the house.

The two wings of the L-shaped structure surround a deck and swimming pool, with a 156-foot sweep of window wall facing south and west and overlooking the pool area. The main section of the house comprises one wing; the second contains a long gallery leading to a guest cabana sited on a promontory closer to the sound. With its panoramic westerly views, this guest cabana, or teahouse, has the feel of a small, separate structure in close touch with the elements. Around the decks and pool, natural stone foundation walls and built-in boulders, imported from the hills around Sun Valley, Idaho, hint at the influence of Japan.

Terry worked with Allen Salsbury on the interiors, with the Stewarts' collection of Asian artifacts and furnishings contributing to the overall effect. One of the most striking pieces is a 36-foot-long Japanese mural that fit perfectly along the wall of the gallery leading to the guest house. Other Asian elements in the original plan of the house included a coffee table made from an antique Thai bed, a pair of sculpted bronze hands from Thailand in a gesture of welcome, antique Japanese panels that served as cabinet doors in the guest room/cabana, and a three-hundred-year-old Buddha figure over the fireplace. In the context of this house, the objects seemed neither contrived nor forced, but rather were all of a piece, shaping with the built-in and custom-designed furnishings, the rich yet understated textures and finishes, and the other elements, a complete and harmonious whole.

Today, the house belongs to Mr. and Mrs. Al Heglund. The Heglunds have installed their own furnishings and have even made some architectural renovations to make the house more suitable for their own needs. Yet its essence remains intact. On entry one feels an almost uncanny sense of grace and ease, brought on by the perfectly realized proportions, the lustrous wood finishes, and the vibrant interplay of East and West as well as of interior and exterior.

The gallery passage, designed to display an Asian mural, connects the guest house or tearoom with the main house.

OPPOSITE: The cast concrete plinths supporting the dark-stained posts were designed after similar ones in a temple in Kyoto. Beyond the glass wall, an intimate garden on the east side of the house flanks the entry gallery.

Remodel of the Raleigh Chinn House

THE RALEIGH CHINN HOUSE was originally designed and constructed in 1905 by the pioneering Seattle Modernist architect Ellsworth Storey, a man responsible for a number of outstanding—and still standing—houses and institutional structures in the Pacific Northwest. Storey has been described as the Northwest's answer to Greene and Greene, one of the best of the Craftsman-style architectural firms to work in the region. Although Terry's more modern inclinations reject the fussier, Victorian-tinged side of Craftsman style, his drive to integrate interiors, furnishings, and architecture into a single, cohesive entity echoes the Craftsman impulse to design and construct everything, both inside and out, in a given project.

The house in question was described in an article in the August 1966 issue of *House & Garden* as a "stately two story wood and stucco house," and like every building it reflected to some extent the customs of its time. Despite the house's history, Roland Terry showed little hesitation in completely remaking it. "It wasn't big enough, so we had to make it right," he says. "And the entry was in the wrong place." In "making it right," Terry brought the house back to life without, in the least, undermining its integrity.

In this house, turn-of-the-century style implied fewer windows and dark, stuffy (by modern standards) interiors to complement the dignified architecture. As is evident in the plan on page 108, Terry's remodel transformed these dark interiors by encircling the original house with a new entrance and circulation gallery, living room, porches, carport, and water features—one inside the house, the other outside. He also turned the plan around, making the former front entrance into a spacious porch and putting in a new front door and entrance, accessed by a pool-spanning footbridge,

Terry expanded a house by architect Ellsworth Storey, adding a glass-walled living room and a new front entry accessed by a footbridge.
Photos: Morley Baer

Morley Baer

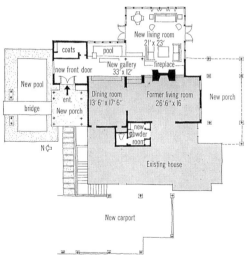

ABOVE: New terraces extend the living space to the exterior. The backyard patio featured a giant chessboard. Plan shows original house surrounded by new rooms and terraces.

OPPOSITE: New interiors included a water feature, far right, and a fireplace topped by a marble slab secured with bronze bolts.

on what was the back of the house. Photographs of the exterior clearly illustrate that the stately bearing of the house was not demeaned in the least: Terry's colorful, gardenlike glass-enclosed living room and the muscular, trellislike rafters of the entrance portico extend like outriggers, opening up the house with forms and details sympathetic to the original architecture, while immeasurably brightening the interior.

The living room represents the boldest break with the past. With three glass walls countered with a single solid wall highlighted by a fireplace, it has what was described at the time as "a profligate sense of openness." Over the fireplace, a slab of travertine marble is secured with decorative bronze bolts. The palette of the furnishings and finishes in this airy new space is all pale and gold, with a white terrazzo floor, white silk folding window screens, and a herringbone ceiling in natural stained cedar. Nothing but glass separates the living room from the adjacent gallery and its reflecting pool, further enhancing the sense of airy spaciousness. In the gallery, Terry placed a bench parallel to the reflecting pool, creating a wonderfully tranquil spot to sit and take in the black slate-framed pool, with its gilded Thai fountainhead gently splashing water over a rock.

A custom-designed marble-topped buffet counter separates the new gallery from the preexisting dining room, allowing the dining room to borrow light from the glass-enclosed gallery. With generous storage capacity, the buffet works as a serving counter from both sides. A new closet inside the entrance provides additional storage space.

Terry is renowned for the elegance of his powder rooms in both homes and restaurants. Here, extending the palette of the house into the powder room, a gold carpet echoed yellow-gold walls and a luminous ceiling, and the faucets, controlled via foot pedals, were built into a brass Buddha sitting atop a marble block on the counter.

At the rear of the house, a black-and-white checked terrace—actually an enormous chessboard—adjoins a new broad-roofed porch, connecting it with the new living room and helping to shape the outdoors into "rooms" that have as much appeal as the indoor volumes they adjoin. The drive to open contact and interplay between the interior and the exterior clearly inspired much of Terry's work on this project. These connections simply did not exist in the original house; Terry's remodel made them integral to the house, and in making them he gave new light and life to a fine old building.

The Roland Terry House

THE TIMELESSNESS OF ROLAND TERRY'S architecture emerges most
powerfully in the house he designed and built for himself on Lopez Island
in the San Juan Islands north of Seattle. Published first in *House Beautiful*
in November 1960 and then again in *Architectural Digest* in June 1989, the
ruggedly elegant house richly expresses many of the ideas and influences
that inspire Terry's work. Though no photographs can do justice to this
magical dwelling tucked among the pines and rocks on a windswept cliff
overlooking Puget Sound, these images do make evident the fact that this is
one of those buildings so appropriately sited and scaled that it feels organic,
as if it grew out of the site rather than having been imposed upon it. And
when you consider the ingredients, the ineffable "rightness," or organic
quality, of the house becomes even more impressive.

Jon Krakauer, writing for *Architectural Digest,* quoted Terry on his feelings
about creating the house: "I think it's immeasurably easier to design a house
for yourself. . . . To tell the truth, this house was one of the most satisfying
projects I've ever done, because I didn't have to answer to anyone but me."
Possibly because no client would consider mixing enormous driftwood logs,
glass walls, old barn siding, sod roofing, and neo-Regence paneling taken
from a demolished Seattle chateau in a small, remote island house. It just
doesn't sound like a good mix. And yet in the sure hands of Roland Terry, it
all fits together.

The architect took his time with his dream house, putting it together
over a period of years, being always careful to respect the site. As he told
Krakauer, "This little corner of the world is very special, . . . the trees have
been growing since the time of the Italian Renaissance. . . . actually, this

Over time, Terry found and hauled to the site
the huge driftwood logs that support the roof
of his retreat on Lopez Island. Everywhere, the
house responds to the site with beautifully
composed views.

was such a magnificent piece of property that it shouldn't have had anything built on it at all. It should have been left in a completely natural state. With that in mind, I made a point of building the house without cutting down any trees, and designed it to intrude on the landscape as little as possible." Actually, Terry admits that he first intended to put the house higher up on the site, because he didn't want to cut down any trees. Then he figured out a design for the lower site that wouldn't require tree cutting, and history was made.

Driftwood logs and massive beams frame the stone fireplace. The furnishings display Terry's light, casually elegant hand as an interior designer.

OPPOSITE: Terry mixed silvery panels from a torn down French-style chateau in Seattle, barn siding, and rugged beams.

OPPOSITE: A sod roof, stone walls, and a trellis of rough beams deepen the house's connection to the terrain. Terry demonstrates an uncanny ability to create a formally organized site and building, while retaining that organic, grounded quality.

The main building plan is quite simple. It consists of a long rectangle subdivided into symmetrical volumes defined by seventeen oversize driftwood structural posts. The uncluttered interior lines and perfectly proportioned rooms recall the work of Andrea Palladio. As Terry noted in *Architectural Digest,* "Palladio is one of my heroes. I've always been interested in classical proportions, especially as they relate to internal volumes."

The house is a marvel of eclectic design. Collected from nearby beaches over a period of years, the posts support a grid of rough beams upon which rests a flat sod roof planted with moss, grasses, and flowers. The interiors contain an inspired mix of elements expressing the Northwest idiom through the generous use of stone, overhanging eaves, and expanses of glass and rough, naturally finished wood. In counterpoint, Terry installed a series of nine-foot-high shuttered French doors around the perimeter of the building. Stripped down to bare wood and stained with ferric chloride, these elaborate doors attained a silvery luster that complements the more natural interiors. The floor consists of concrete aggregate with a design by James Wegner, inspired by swirling tidal waters. The furnishings also reflect Terry's fearless approach to design. Antiques, custom-designed pieces, and understated, off-the-shelf items mingle with artwork from all over the world, while plentiful light and a practical floorplan shape a pleasing, comfortable mix of indoor and outdoor spaces.

Textiles designer Jack Lenor Larsen unabashedly states that this house should be made into an architectural museum, while Seattle architect William Bain, a partner in the architectural firm NBBJ, favorably compares it to Taliesin East, Frank Lloyd Wright's masterwork home in Spring Green, Wisconsin. Terry no longer owns the property, but the visual record clearly establishes this house as one of the great residential projects of the Northwest. In himself, Terry clearly found the ideal client.

The Carpinteria House

BY THE END OF THE 1980S ROLAND TERRY'S career had begun to
wind down, and his residential projects became fewer in number. At the
same time, his designs took on a minimalist dignity, an utterly assured simplicity, as the influence of Andrea Palladio grew stronger. Working in collaboration with Jean Jongeward, a former associate who had gone on to
create a notable career for herself as an interior designer, Terry created one
of his last great residential projects on a sunny, ocean-view hilltop in Carpinteria, in Southern California. The home was featured in *Architectural Digest*
in April 1993.

This house in Southern California exhibits
a more formal, Palladian-influenced style,
appropriate to the Mediterranean clime.

One half of the client couple hailed from the Northwest, and the family
had summered in an old Victorian farmhouse on the 60-acre ranchland site
for a number of years. When they decided to build a new house on the
property, rather than expand the original home, they elected to build atop
a hill, to expand their view. Jean Jongeward had designed interiors for them
previously, and it was through her that they met Roland Terry. The couple
then paid a visit to Terry's house on Lopez Island and discovered a sympathetic design spirit. The husband was quoted in *Architectural Digest:* "We vis-
ited his house in the San Juans, and when I walked up to it and saw the sod
roof, I thought, this is a little too earthy for me. But when I walked inside,
I realized that Terry was doing exactly what we hoped to do. The combination of driftwood pillars and 18th century walnut paneling convinced me
he could balance the rough with the classical." They explained to Terry that
what they wanted was "the carriage house to a Palladian villa." Their needs
were simple: two bedrooms, a kitchen, a dining room, and a large, square
common room, surrounded by gardens designed as outdoor rooms.

TOP AND BOTTOM LEFT: Terry ringed the house with a series of gardens and gathering places designed as outdoor rooms.

TOP RIGHT: The dining area flows out onto adjacent terraces. The house demonstrates a fine balance of the rough and the classical. California light allows for a subdued palette.

Interior designer Jean Jongeward collaborated with Terry in creating the interiors, which feature casually elegant contemporary furnishings set off against the refined roughness of the finishes.

For an architect steeped in the traditions of Northwest design, the dry, scrubby terrain of Southern California represented an entirely different kind of challenge. And yet Terry's cosmopolitan view—coupled with a recent visit to the Po Valley in Italy—had, in a sense, prepared him for the task. As he said at the time, "The site has a wonderful outlook. That kind of hogback, looking in both directions, is very Italianate, and I understood at once that they envisioned a country ranch house with some fairly dramatic living space." Terry turned to Palladio: "The marvel of Palladio's designs is that they were extremely simple—boxes, really—but beautifully proportioned."

And so a Palladian box arose on a Carpinteria hilltop. The palette is neutral; the details—a round, pantheonlike front hall, a stone fireplace, an intricate wood ceiling—are spare yet infused with classical grace. Jongeward's interior palette and furniture selections reflect the same subdued tones, coupled with a willingness to mix and match styles that appears to have been inspired by the fearless eclecticism of her mentor, Roland Terry. They include stone and hardwood floors, textured rugs, and furniture ranging from contemporary metal tables to eighteenth-century chairs to bookcases retrofitted into antique door surrounds.

The building is surrounded by grass and paved patios that serve as elegant outdoor rooms. Coupled with panoramic views, these outdoor rooms set up an intriguing dialogue between inside and outside, between the intimate and the spectacular. Effortlessly evoking Palladio, celebrating the Southern California light, and encapsulating many of the ideas and concerns that inspired the architect over the decades, the house represents "a successful pairing of setting and style." Noted Terry in *Architectural Digest*, "It's become one of my favorite houses."

A circular rotunda with a stair rising to the second story adds a formal note.

OPPOSITE: A trellised promenade of grapevines screens an intimate garden, one of the house's several outdoor rooms. Photo: © John Vaughan, Photographer. © 2000 The Condé Nast Publications Inc. All rights reserved. Used with permission.

The Andrew House

ONE OF TERRY'S LAST MAJOR residential projects was a house for Lucius and Phoebe Andrew in the Highlands, a gated residential community in north Seattle. Designed in the 1990s to replace an earlier house on the site, the Andrew residence is a somewhat formal, Palladian-influenced Northwest villa, beautifully positioned in the midst of expansive green lawns, with a variety of mature trees and ornamental shrubbery surrounding the house with layers of softening greenery. The client requested a large house, and although it doesn't appear bulky or voluminous—Terry's design neatly integrates the two-story building into the sloping landscape—it is a surprisingly large, rambling structure. Approached via a long, curving driveway, the one-story entry side of the house presents a fairly formal facade, with pillars flanking the front door, which is framed within a generously scaled bank of windows screened for privacy with louvers.

One end of the villa—the "private" wing—expands to two stories as it descends the slope, providing space for guest rooms, offices, and a master suite with balconies on one level, and more bedrooms, recreation rooms, and offices below. With an enormous living room positioned behind the entry gallery at the center of the structure, the "public" wing, extending in the opposite direction, includes a formal dining room, kitchen, large family room off the kitchen, and various pantries and service rooms. Terraces and formal gardens flow off the back of the house; in particular, a formally organized terrace lies off the dining room and the family room, providing an easily accessed outdoor gathering space sheltered beneath a muscular trellis planted with shade-making vines.

© 1999 Donna Day

A formal sheltered terrace provides an outdoor gathering place at the Andrew house.

OPPOSITE: As it descends the sloping site, the house expands to two stories on one end. Terry placed the master suite on the upstairs corner with a spacious balcony overlooking the grounds, which are planted with a variety of mature trees and shrubbery. Photo: © 1999 Donna Day

Terry's design includes a formal, symmetrical entry facade, with the double doors flanked by pillars. Louvers provide privacy for the entry gallery.

Terry here crafted a large, luxurious home with a finely balanced mix of formal and informal elements, private and public areas, and indoor and outdoor rooms. For all its vast and rambling spaces, as is true with all of Terry's residential projects, the Andrew house is above all comfortable and user-friendly, designed in response to the needs of its owners.

Adjacent to the dining room and the family room,
this trellis-shaded terrace serves as an outdoor
dining room. Boxwood hedges organize the
gardens that encircle much of the house.

Washington Park Tower

FROM THE BEGINNING, controversy swirled around Terry's Washington Park Tower project. Such controversy was inevitable, given the nature of the building: a twenty-three-story high-rise condominium on the ultimate low-rise site, the shore of a lake in a residential neighborhood composed primarily of single-family homes. In a June 1967 *Seattle Magazine* profile of Terry, he was quoted defending the tower with these words: "What we have to avoid is the five or six-storied low-rise apartments that have ruined Capitol Hill. They're the slums of tomorrow, and they also wall off the lake. What has to come is tall, slender towers that permit plenty of parkland and view." One is reminded of a similar project that never got off Frank Lloyd Wright's drawing board: his penultimate residential structure, a mile-high apartment building, surrounded by acres of greensward. Though far more grandiose, Wright's concept is not that different from Terry's notion here.

Terry's tower still stands, and the high prices of 1967—$33,000 to $100,000 for a one- to three-bedroom condo—seem laughably low now, especially for a bird's-eye perch in one of the great view buildings of the Seattle area. The building was designed so that no unit had views into any other unit, lending each the quality of a freestanding "home in the sky."

It is hard to judge the building objectively. Terry believed other tall buildings would follow in the area and give some appropriate scale to this first one. Yet even without high-rise neighbors to put it in context, the tower does have a certain grace, an ease of composition imposed by the balance of horizontal and vertical elements. The unbroken planes of the vertical walls extending out create an intriguing angularity and lend a kind of openness to the structure. Also, the original plans called for sheathing the tower in copper, which would have given it a more elegant, interesting patina. All things considered, the Washington Park Tower remains a successful project, one of Terry's most ambitious buildings, appreciated especially by those with the good fortune to live inside.

OPPOSITE: Terry's only high-rise project, the Washington Park Tower, rose on the shore of Lake Washington in the 1960s. Vertical panels, center and right, create privacy for every unit in the building.

127

Current Terry Residence

ROLAND TERRY MOVED into his current residence, near the town of Mt. Vernon in Washington State's Skagit Valley, in 1992. Located amid expansive fields of raspberries, tulips, and daffodils, the property includes the house, a new wooden building sheltering an indoor swimming pool, and an existing barn for storage. Terry completely redesigned the old country farmhouse and property to accommodate his personal requirements, including his magnificent collection of artwork, antiques, custom-designed furniture, and unusual objects.

Prior to the renovation, the house and an adjacent two-car garage were approached from the road via a driveway that led directly to the front door. In his new plan for the property, Terry moved the driveway away from the front of the house and shifted the parking area to the rear. He fenced the front yard and turned it into a sheltered lawn and patio area. He then transformed the existing two-car garage into an airy, high-ceilinged living room and connected it to the original house by a new light-filled, tile-floored indoor garden gallery. He moved the main entrance—marked with a signature Roland Terry metal-clad door—to the back of the living room (the former garage) and created a sheltered outdoor corridor, flanking the new pool house, to connect the new rear parking area with the new entrance. After installing a custom-designed French limestone fireplace on one wall to create a focal point, Terry decorated the new living room with an eclectic assortment of furnishings, light fixtures, paintings, and sculptures designed or specified for various projects and/or gathered during his travels around the world.

Air Photo Inc.

Roland Terry's current residence in the Skagit Valley includes the house, a new wooden building sheltering an indoor swimming pool, and an existing barn for storage.

OPPOSITE: Terry transformed a two-car garage into a comfortable living room with rich red walls and a custom-designed French limestone fireplace. Terry designed the chairs in the foreground. The piece over the fireplace, from India, was a gift from Anne Gould Hauberg. The hanging light fixture was originally designed by Irene McGowan for Terry's house on Lopez Island.

Photo: © 2000 Donna Day

One wall in the den features a multisheet antique street map of Paris, purchased by Roland Terry during his European travels. Terry painted the den floor with a checkerboard pattern to echo the map. As illustrated here, the house is full of riches: a chair from China, a horse from Togoland, a Peruvian statue, and paintings by Abdelwahid Elhassan (on the table) and Florence Beach Terry (upper left). The small chest on the tabletop at left dates from the sixteenth century.

The house's original living room, lined with books and artifacts accumulated over half a century of collecting, now serves as Terry's study. To open up this space, Terry took down the wall that separated it from the existing dining room, transforming the two small rooms into a single, large volume, with their separate functions defined by furnishings and changes in finish and texture, such as the lively checkerboard pattern painted on the original wood flooring in the den. In all three of these warm, comfortable rooms—indeed throughout the house—Terry has created a wonderfully appealing environment, perfectly attuned to the needs of a retired architect with impeccable taste in art, furnishings, and accessories.

LEFT: Terry originally designed the rawhide-covered chest for the Paul Roland Smith house in the 1950s (see pp. 32–35). Mrs. Smith later gave it to him. The painting above the chest is a view of Puget Sound by Terry's mother, Florence Beach Terry.

RIGHT: A light-filled garden gallery connects the new living room with the former living room, which has been transformed into a den.

COMMERCIAL WORK

ROLAND TERRY'S TALENT FOR MAKING COMFORTABLE, elegantly proportioned spaces, simultaneously inspired by the site and designed "from the inside out," served him well as he expanded his work in the commercial realm in the decades after 1960. With long-term associates such as Carol Bain, Jim Mayeno, Robert Egan, and other employees and collaborators, Terry took on a diverse array of projects, primarily in the hospitality arena but including retail, institutional, civic, and office buildings as well.

The existing visual record of this work is spotty; however, by combing through photos, articles, plans, and especially Terry's many fine drawings and watercolors, one can obtain a sense of the colorful and varied nonresidential work, both built and unbuilt, created by the firm. Some of these projects still exist in much the same form as shown here; others have been drastically remodeled, expanded, or torn down, or were never built. Terry's commercial and institutional portfolio demonstrates the ways he adapted his unique design skills to the requirements of restaurants, office buildings, civic and institutional buildings and complexes, and especially hotels in a wide range of locales ranging from urban to suburban to rural wilderness. As is especially evident in the hotels, Terry always looked to local design motifs and traditions to lend a sense of identity to projects. At the same time, he brought his own original interpretations of Northwest Modernist idioms to bear on everything he designed. "Hotels are interesting if you have the money to bring in some first-rate artists," he says. "Then it can be interesting and really fun." As noted on a Terry and Egan brochure, he almost always designed the whole package: "This is one of the first firms in the USA to establish an interior design department as an integral and mandatory part of architectural planning. The total concept—Integrated architecture, interior design and landscape design—is and always has been the rule."

The Hilton Inn

LOCATED NEAR SEATAC AIRPORT, the Hilton Inn represents one of Terry's early efforts at integrating Northwest regional materials and motifs into a large-scale nonresidential project. The five buildings in the motor hotel complex were designed by Skidmore Owings and Merrill. After being "accosted by a New York interior designer looking for help with the project," Terry's office contributed designs for the courtyards and landscape, and selected interior finishes, furnishings, and artwork for the main lobby building, which contained the lobby, lobby lounge, and banquet and dining rooms. Collaborators included Peter Canlis, food-service consultant, Irene McGowan, lighting designer, and several local artists, among them sculptor James Wegner and painter Guy Anderson. Terry recalls that without insisting on anything, "we would ask the artists to do something, and if you can suggest a Northwest mode, it would be good."

Published in *Institutions Magazine* in 1961, the hotel's interiors demonstrate Terry's skill at adapting rugged native materials to projects requiring sophistication as well as more complicated space planning. The Montana slate floors, rough-cut timbers, and especially the Northwest-inspired artworks lend the hotel a strong sense of regional identity, deftly balancing luxury and informality while offering guests a taste of regional style. The property's most striking feature is an indoor-outdoor patio with pine trees, sculptures, and fountains splashing into a pool, visually connected via glass walls to the lobby, yet open to the sky—a little piece of the great Northwest (with intimations of Japan) built into the most public space in the hotel.

Wood, stone, and regionally inspired artwork place the hotel in a Northwest context.

In response to a state law requiring that cocktail lounges not be visible from the street, Terry shielded the lounge behind a stone wall decorated with mosaic tile inserts, providing an opaque yet visually stimulating counterpoint to the transparent view into the inner courtyard. Throughout the public spaces, the designers and artists employed a warm, earthy palette to further enhance the regional identity of the hotel. Aware of the high traffic demands of hotels, Terry planned for practicality as well as aesthetics: the stone floors are sealed and virtually maintenance free; deep pile carpets are inset into the floors to eliminate wear on the edges; doors are surfaced in linen, then laminated in plastic.

As is evident in the few photos extant, even in the programmatic confines of a hotel lobby and dining areas, Terry engaged in a dialogue between ruggedness and elegance, between simplicity and luxury, between intimacy and grandeur, between transparency and opacity. The integration of these ostensibly opposing elements into such appealing, comfortable environments always lends a level of intrigue to Terry's work.

ABOVE AND OPPOSITE: An elegantly lit indoor garden creates a dramatic, Asian-styled centerpiece off the lobby and bar of the Hilton Inn, near SeaTac Airport. Photos: Chas. R. Pearson

The Kahala Hilton Hotel

TERRY'S WORK ON THIS HAWAIIAN RESORT demonstrates his ability to collaborate with both architects and interior designers, for on this project his niche lay between the two, and required that he do both architecture and interior design, integrating structure and decor, building out an architect's interior shell while making room for the furnishings and finishes applied by another designer. In doing so, he successfully applied his personal interpretation of Northwest Style in a completely different context—the Kahala Hilton, a bastion of tropical elegance in a posh Honolulu suburb, ten minutes from the heavily-touristed heart of Waikiki Beach.

According to historic lore, Conrad Hilton's intention with the Kahala was to re-create, in 1964, the serenity and style of the classic Royal Hawaiian Hotel that had flourished before Waikiki boomed. The architecture featured reinforced concrete in muted tones, to blend with the surrounding terrain. An elaborate series of pools, fountains, and islands lent the property a lush tropical ambience, while extensive plantings surrounding the building integrated it into the land- and waterscape. By constructing part of the building on stilts—and then extending the stilts upward in a trellislike superstructure around the entire exterior, the designer enhanced the garden effect and downscaled the mass of the twelve-story guestroom tower.

Quickly emerging as the hotel of choice for celebrities from every walk of life, the soon-to-be-nicknamed "Kahollywood Hilton" had a long run as a popular Hawaiian destination. A period of decline followed, until the hotel was purchased by the Mandarin Oriental group, which remodeled and expanded the property in the early 1990s.

The Kahala Hilton, now the Kahala Mandarin Oriental, ten minutes from Waikiki Beach, has been a favorite Honolulu hotel since opening in the 1960s.

137

This photo illustrates the Kahala's main lobby during the 1960s. Terry created the interior architecture, including the chandeliers by Irene McGowan, but he did not design or specify the furnishings.

A comparison of two photographs of the hotel's magnificent 80-foot-long, 30-foot-high lobby reveals how little the space has changed. The photo on this page, from the mid-1960s, features the original interior architecture and design by Roland Terry, Robert Egan, Irene McGowan, decorator David Williams, and their assorted collaborators and associates. The other, on page 139, from the late 1990s, shows the hotel after it was extensively renovated with new interior designs from Hirsch Bedner Associates, a Los Angeles–based design firm.

Looking past the furniture groupings in both photographs, it is clear

that Hirsch Bedner's designers hardly touched the essence of Terry's interior architecture—the pale, tropical version of his exposed post-and-beam structure; the sand and beige palette; the tall, louvered windows, reminiscent of old Hawaiian plantation houses; the abundant plantings; and above all, the chandeliers and other light fixtures, designed for the original lobby. Constructed of oxidized metal and fused glass—like the sea glass one picks up on the beach—the three chandeliers weigh over a ton each. Over the decades they have become icons, much-loved symbols of the Kahala spirit, and are symbolic of the timelessness of the original design as well.

A view of the same space from the late 1990s shows how Terry's interior architecture, including the chandeliers, remains intact, although the furnishings have been completely replaced.

The Doubletree Inn, Seattle

IN 1970, INSTALLING A WOOD-FINISHED, contemporary country inn–style motor hotel among the glass and concrete buildings of South-center, a formerly rural area developed into shopping malls, made perfect sense. It gave the wives of young business travelers—the target market for this property—a Northwest-inspired "shopping base" to enjoy while their husbands went into Seattle on business. Although today the notion of Southcenter having anything to do with "the country" is long gone, the Doubletree Inn remains a successful regional hotel today and a popular destination for meetings and conventions.

Terry's design, which earned him the Institutions Award of Special Distinction for interior design from *Institutions Magazine* in June 1970, was completed on a moderate budget and displays his usual sense of complete integration, with the interior finishes and furnishings seamlessly coordinated with the architecture. The primary material is natural wood, with furnishings, fixtures, accessories, and artwork specified in earthy colors and rich textures to complement the wood and enhance the warm appeal of the interiors. Terry's signature exposed structural posts and heavy beams can be seen throughout, lending rugged regional authenticity; in the hotel's Boojum Tree restaurant, these rough elements are balanced by elegant linens and simple white dishes. Inspired by regional motifs, artist James Wegner created a number of pieces for the property, including an entire wall of wood sculptures inspired by Native American storage boxes.

Terry tailored the property for meetings and incorporated into every meeting room those elements discovered to be important in a survey of planners: a coat room, counters, storage, blackboards, projection screens, and soundproofing to ensure privacy.

Anticipating later trends in hotel design, Terry installed warm light fixtures in the hotel corridors—traditionally an alienating and unpleasant area in hotels. He also designed Native American motifs to be woven into carpets to enliven the corridors and to signal the location of guest room doors. Individual room–controlled air conditioning and heating was another innovation here, as were patio doors providing guests with direct access to the hotel's pool and secluded courtyards. The hotel has been updated several times since opening, but the essence of the design remains intact, and many of the innovative aspects of this project have helped set new, user-friendly standards for hospitality design.

Natural wood and exposed structural elements lend regional charm to the Doubletree Inn near Seattle.

OPPOSITE: Ground-floor rooms open onto patios with direct access to the pool.

The Doubletree Inn, Phoenix

IN CONTRAST WITH THE LOW-RISE RAMBLE of the Doubletree Inn in Seattle, the Phoenix property is a ten-story contemporary urban tower with a striking glass and concrete exterior, enhanced with a captivating illumination plan that, by night, transforms the two wings of the tower into a monumental light sculpture. Terry created the property in collaboration with Phoenix architects Peter Lendrum and Associates. The mass of the tower appears surprisingly "light on its feet," due to the fine-tuned balance of horizontal and vertical elements and the interplay of glass and concrete— signature Terry stylistic devices writ large on a different horizon, that of the wide-open Southwest.

Terry's talent for knitting disparate elements together to achieve appealing effects emerges here as well. Positioned in front of the distinctly urban guestroom tower, the hotel's destination high-end restaurant, the Boojum Tree, features a low-profile one-story exterior clad in barnboards, its rough-hewn appearance dynamically contrasting with the tower. With heavy yet graceful posts and beams echoing the exterior interplay of horizontal and vertical, the contrast continues inside: lobby areas are paneled in rough hemlock and decorated with landscapes to enhance the "country" ambience. A boldly geometric carpet, counterpointed with tile floors, evokes Southwest Native American graphic designs; restaurant upholstery, wall decorations, and other elements also enhance the ethnic/regional identity of the project. Absorbing and interpreting appropriate motifs wherever he worked, Terry created buildings that were distinctly his, yet always grounded in their location.

Chas. R. Pearson

The Boojum Tree restaurant at the Doubletree Inn, Phoenix, features graphic designs inspired by Southwest Native American motifs.

OPPOSITE: The hotel features a double-wing tower with a striking illumination plan.
Photo: Chas. R. Pearson

Sun Mountain Lodge

IN HIS EARLY 1960S DESIGN for the highly regarded and still-thriving Sun Mountain Lodge, perched atop a hill a thousand feet above the Methow Valley in Eastern Washington, Roland Terry turned his talents to the decidedly rural. The once-rustic lodge has been updated in recent years to accommodate a perhaps more pampered, less spartan crowd, but its rugged, site-inspired architectural essence remains unchanged. These photographs from the 1960s reveal a self-effacing, site-sensitive structure that looks much the same today, several decades after original construction.

Terry began work on this project by walking the terrain extensively with the developer. He then organized the site, situating the restaurant and bar on the north side of the building to maximize the dramatic views across the Methow Valley and into the North Cascades. As is evident in the photographs, the low-rise, stone and wood structure closely follows the contours of the mountains, its profile virtually disappearing when silhouetted against the magnificent peaks towering overhead.

Working with local contractors, Terry created a strong structure, intentionally very rough, with blunt beams and intriguing roof shapes. The building was simple, with generously scaled decks and fireplaces, and crude railings and beams, all cut different ways and with saw whiskers everywhere. He used exposed aggregate, concrete, and plywood—rough materials—to make rich spaces, and then picked the perfect furnishings for them.

Quietly hugging its contoured hilltop at the foot of the North Cascades' powerful peaks, Sun Mountain Lodge, in both its original form and its new, upscale incarnation, remains a remarkable piece of environmental architecture, a work of lasting value in a rugged, timelessly beautiful location.

At Sun Mountain Lodge, Terry used stone walls to organize the outdoor hot tub and swimming pool.

OPPOSITE: The rough-hewn outpost is constructed of raw logs with generous windows.
Photo: Don Portman

Don Portman

Don Portman

TOP AND OPPOSITE: Winter and summer, the lodge hugs its rounded ridgetop site, disappearing into a vast, ruggedly dramatic landscape.

BOTTOM: Terry's interiors for the lodge were intentionally made rough-and-ready, with log posts and beams, stone walls, and leather and wood seating.

The Halekulani Hotel

IN 1982, AFTER A PERIOD OF DECLINE, the new owners of the popular Halekulani Hotel, an institution on Waikiki Beach, commissioned an architectural expansion of the property from the California firm of Killingsworth Stricker Lindgren & Wilson. The idea was to transform the venerable 199-room hotel into a 456-room resort without sacrificing the low-key, high-end charm that had always defined the Halekulani. The new ownership-management team hired Terry and Egan to work with the architects on a complete redesign of the property's interior architecture and design.

The new plan included a near-total demolition of the existing hotel property, followed by reconstruction of the original low-rise main building. Additionally, the architecture and design teams developed several new buildings—multistory ramblers, according to Robert Egan—with new interior architecture and decorative elements for all the spaces. The Terry and Egan design team took its cues from Polynesian and other Asian Pacific motifs, specifying fabrics and other elements based on traditional island designs. Terry describes the outcome as "Polynesian residential." This is evident in the finishes and furnishings, and even in the names of the rooms—the "Living Room," for example, where the designers achieved a high-end residential effect in a plantation-colonial mode. But the scale of the spaces is much grander, with high ceilings supported by muscular posts and beams. Here, as we have so often seen in Terry's work, these structural elements are left exposed. They serve to help organize the volumes and to frame wonderful views of the sea: Diamond Head down the beach and, on a more intimate scale, the gardens and landscapes of the hotel property. The interaction of inside and outside comes into play here as well, with several primary public

In expanding and renovating the Halekulani Hotel on Waikiki Beach, Terry maintained the quiet residential charm of the original and new low-rise rambling buildings (opposite) with residential-scale furnishings and detailing in interiors, as in the Living Room (above).

TOP: Drawing shows how new guest-room towers flank the expanded original structures.

spaces left open to adjacent gardens or patios, separated by louvered doors or screens for use in inclement weather.

Robert Egan has continued to replace elements and refine the design in the years since, but most of the original design from the early 1980s remains in place. Many critics still rank the Halekulani among the finest hotels in the world, an opinion substantiated by *Gourmet* magazine's 1999 readers' poll, which put it at the top, naming the Halekulani the number one hotel in the world.

ABOVE AND OPPOSITE, BOTTOM: The designers employed a casually elegant, residential-style approach to the interiors, with an emphasis on views and inside-outside living.

Las Torres Restaurant

FOR LAS TORRES RESTAURANT, Terry's design team specified bright colors, Mexican decorative accessories, and colorful furnishings to lend this Tucson dining room a festive air—one that presaged the "Tex-Mex" southwestern theme that was so prevalent in the 1980s and 1990s. Named for the small towers atop the building, Las Torres was created out of an existing structure—a private residence—with the addition of a new wing to house the main dining room inside and provide a long, shaded entry porch, or gallery, outside. Made of worn, naturally finished wood, the beamed ceilings, peeled-log interior elements, and exterior trellises—all transplanted Northwest elements—neatly blend with the hand-worked plaster, rounded corners, bright colors, and other southwestern motifs.

A spacious shaded entry patio and colorful interior illustrate the influence of southwestern and Mexican design on Terry's work at the Las Torres Restaurant in Tucson, a residence converted into a restaurant.

153

Canlis Restaurants, Portland and San Francisco

AFTER DESIGNING RESTAURANTS for the Canlis family in Seattle and Waikiki Beach, Terry and his associates went on to do Canlis restaurants in Portland, Oregon, and San Francisco. For the creation of the Canlis Restaurant in Portland, in the 1960s, its location atop the Hilton Hotel permitted the designers to employ slanting glass walls like those first used in the Seattle Canlis. Counterpointing the transparency of these expansive view walls, the Canlis trademark elements—subtle "island" motifs along with wood and stone—create the appealing balance of rusticity and elegance that serve as the restaurant's trademark. With its lavish plantings and elaborate stonework, the entry is perhaps the most striking aspect of the Portland Canlis.

The San Francisco Canlis was installed in the 1970s in the Fairmont Hotel, one of the city's finest accommodations, with an entrance on California Street. It was, says Terry, "an important affair," with a lounge, private dining rooms, and a high-end ambience enhanced with a fine array of artwork. The San Francisco Canlis, with its urban, ground-floor location, does not feature the expansive glass walls and inside-outside interaction of earlier Canlis spaces, but instead, for the most part, turns in on itself, with a sophisticated illumination system highlighting the extensive art collection. Yet as is evident in the photographs, San Francisco shares with the other Canlis restaurants the refined use of natural wood and stone, trademarks developed by Tucker, Shields, and Terry in the original Canlis restaurant in the late 1940s. Generally speaking, the Canlis restaurants established the idea that a "chain" of high-end restaurants could work in different locations. Terry's designs, with their subtle adjustments to locale underscored by the motifs and materials shared by all, had much to do with the restaurants' success.

At the rooftop Canlis in Portland (opposite), Terry specified the same floor-to-ceiling slanted windows as Seattle's Canlis. In San Francisco's Canlis (above), wall-size murals replace the view windows.

Seattle Center

IN THE AFTERMATH OF THE 1962 Seattle World's Fair, Roland Terry was
one of the architects asked by the powers-that-be in the City of Seattle to
explore various ways to build on the fair's momentum and keep the Seattle
Center active as a viable part of the urban fabric. As is evident from the large
number of drawings and photographs that document the site, Terry and his
associates envisioned myriad new indoor and outdoor venues for the areas in
and around the Center House building. Their plans for the food circus were
realized, and this popular eatery, with its glowing central fountain, remains a
lively part of the city. Nearby, on the same world's fair campus, Terry planned
a section of the Opera House lobby to incorporate a Mark Tobey mural, a
gift to the city from the John Hauberg family.

After the world's fair in 1962, Terry contrib-
uted numerous ideas for continued use of
Seattle Center, including renovating the
Opera House lobby.

St. Mark's Cathedral

ALTHOUGH THEY REMAIN UNREALIZED, Terry's drawings for the restoration and renovation of St. Mark's Cathedral on Seattle's Capitol Hill exhibit an appropriately understated approach to reworking this dignified and architecturally significant religious building.

Interior and exterior views of Terry's unbuilt scheme for renovating St. Mark's Cathedral, a landmark church on Seattle's Capitol Hill.

Nordstrom

PRIOR TO THE CONSTRUCTION of this first major Nordstrom store in downtown Seattle, the retailer had occupied two lesser buildings in the same block, with a number of smaller buildings positioned between them—"bad little buildings," in Roland Terry's words. And so, in the 1970s, Terry and Egan teamed up with designers from Skidmore Owings and Merrill's San Francisco office to create one unified space. The firms jointly designed the various interior departments as well as the exterior of this monolithic, yet elegant, department store.

Some admirers of Roland Terry consider the Nordstrom building to have been one of his more difficult designs. Others—especially those still enamored of unalloyed Modernism—admired the spartan clarity of the boxy white structure. Beneath the step-down canopy, edged in festive Tivoli-style lights, the store's windows established appealing visual rhythms, neatly displaying merchandise according to department store requirements. Above the canopy, in the warming glow of uplights, the building's pale exterior, enhanced with a subtle interplay of horizontal and vertical elements, commanded Seattle's retail downtown until late 1999—a long, successful run in the finicky, fiercely competitive business of retail.

OPPOSITE: Terry united a motley assemblage of small, undistinguished storefronts and buildings to create the original, coolly modern Nordstrom building in downtown Seattle.

AMFAC

IN THE 1970S, ROLAND TERRY created an imaginative and innovative office design for the San Francisco financial holding company AMFAC. The interior focuses on an indoor garden surrounding a central pool; offices ring the garden, which is illuminated by a ceiling grid of alternating solids and skylights supported by concrete beams. The grid creates dramatic natural light effects on the garden below; the solid elements in the grid also subtly echo the rectangular steps Terry arrayed in a random pattern over and around the pool. Countering the rectilinearity of these ceiling and floor elements, the plantings, including ferns, bright green groundcovers, and numerous tall, leafy trees, join with the pools and fountains to establish a serene, organic ambience. The abstract green-and-white tile design on the bottom of the pool, shaped into curves that suggest the movement of water, further this natural quality and enhance the creeklike effect—an effect deepened by the placement of the steps and the irregular shape of the pool. The company's offices surround this water feature, with glass walls looking "out" into the central garden. With its outside-inside emphasis on natural light, simple materials, and organic energy, the AMFAC office presages the kind of ecologically correct, naturally lit space that has emerged as a major design trend in the late 1990s.

OPPOSITE: Water and myriad plantings lend a natural, organic quality to the AMFAC offices Terry designed in San Francisco. The skylight patterns are echoed in the irregular steps across the water features. Photo: © Chan Young

Bank of California

THE BANK OF CALIFORNIA PROJECT in downtown Seattle offered Terry and Egan the opportunity to apply a regionally inspired approach to a major interior architecture program. This 1970s project consisted of a complete build-out of multiple floors of public, semipublic, and private office spaces for a major financial institution. The designers carefully programmed the space on every floor and then employed natural wood finishes and architecturally integrated lighting to create a warm, inviting ambience. Finally, the installation of Northwest Coast Native American iconography and imagery as decorative highlights served to establish a vital connection between this out-of-state corporation and its Northwest home. From Terry's point of view the important thing to note is that he approached this major commercial project in the same fashion he approached a residential project; that is, he sought to create a comfortable, user-friendly space, with low maintenance and long-lived materials, so that the design would last—literally and thematically.

The Bank of California building in downtown Seattle features Northwest-inspired natural wood finishes and Northwest Coast Native American art to tie the out-of-state corporation to the region. Photos: © 1974 Chas. R. Pearson

Marco Polo Bookstore

IN THE MID-1990S TERRY ACCOMPLISHED space planning, interior design, and decoration for the Marco Polo Bookstore. Located in a Capitol Hill building originally designed by noted Seattle architect Arthur L. Loveless, the store specializes in travel books and accessories. Terry's choice of the evocative, desert-toned palette was inspired by the store's namesake, wanderer Marco Polo, and his travels through Asia.

Terry reorganized the floorplan, rearranging portals and passageways to create a more functional circulation pattern that allows patrons to browse through an unhurried circuit of the store's four rooms. He also designed the millwork, bookshelves, counters, and merchandise display areas. The most striking elements in the store are a pair of murals commissioned by Terry from Native American artist Leo Adams. The murals suggest Asian painting styles; at the same time, they evoke imaginary realms—the places travelers visit in their dreams. Coupled with a fireplace, casual, comfortable furnishings, and a soothing palette, the murals provide the perfect backdrop for the many intriguing books and objects on display, establishing in this retail space a civilized, multilayered ambience not so very different from one of Roland Terry's richly appealing residential interiors.

For the Marco Polo travel bookstore in Seattle's Capitol Hill neighborhood, Terry commissioned two murals from Native American artist Leo Adams; they face each other across the main room, shown above and at left.

Photos: © 2000 Donna Day

167

Project Committee's Acknowledgments

Just as it is important for the artists of a region to be published, it is important to recognize the contributions of architects, and one of the most important and influential to subsequent generations of architects and interior designers in this region is Roland Terry. In recognition of this, the committee set out to publish this monograph. We are fortunate that the University of Washington Press, directed by Pat Soden, has taken such an active interest in the architecture and architectural history of the Pacific Northwest.

The project was greatly advanced by the existence of a fund created by the Trustees of the Guendolen Carkeek Plestcheeff Decorative Arts Institute. In 1997 the Trustees of the Institute transferred funds to the Corporate Council for the Arts to create the Guendolen Carkeek Plestcheeff Decorative and Design Arts Fund, and this has provided the initial substantial funding for this project. A major grant from the Bagley Wright Foundation supplemented that fund. A little committee made up of Peter Donnelly, Anne Gould Hauberg, Herbert Hall, Laura Ingham, Merrill Wright, and Virginia Wyman steered the project to publication and worked with gifted designer Ed Marquand to see it to fruition. That committee would like to thank the following contributors who made this possible.

Ralph Anderson

Phoebe H. Andrew

Bill and Carol Bain

Fred Bassetti, FAIA, NA

Mr. and Mrs. John M. Baxter

David C. Black

Kathlyn E. (Betty) Black

T. William Booth

Corporate Council for the Arts Guendolen Carkeek Plestcheeff
    Decorative and Design Arts Fund

Peter F. Donnelly

Mr. and Mrs. E. Peter Garrett

Anne Gould Hauberg

Sharon and Brad Ingham

Frederick and Susan Ingham

Kip and Marsha Ingham

Laura Ingham

Charmly and Tucker Ingham

William P. and Ruth Ingham

Sue Justen

Alan C. Liddle

Richard D. Lindstrom

Frederic and Kate Lyman

John F. Nesholm

Anne Parry

William G. and Victoria Reed, Jr. Kalakala Point Foundation

Gladys and Sam Rubinstein Foundation

Kayla Skinner

Paul W. Skinner

Margaret P. Taylor

George and Colleen Willoughby

The Bagley Wright Fund

Wyman Youth Trust

Author's Acknowledgments

In pursuit of understanding Roland Terry and his career as an architect I am indebted to many individuals. First and foremost, I would like to thank Roland himself for the time he put into gathering materials, showing me projects, and discussing the work he has accomplished over the past fifty years. Thanks also to Abdelwahid Elhassan for search and rescue of renderings, drawings, articles, and photographs of Roland Terry's work, long lost in the big red barn; and for his unstinting friendship and selfless devotion to Roland's health and well-being. Thanks to all the writers of the magazine articles about Roland's work from the 1940s to the 1990s; these pieces made my own job less difficult. Thanks to Ralph Anderson, Phoebe Andrew, William Bain, Carol Bain, Marcella Benditt, Michael Cunningham, Mark Daniels, Robert Egan, Anne Gould Hauberg, John Hauberg, Al Heglund, David Hewitt, Warren Hill, Laura Ingham, Jim Mayeno, Jennifer Naimy, Jim Olson, Allen Vance Salsbury, Marvell Stewart, and George Suyama (and any others I may have spoken with and failed to mention here) for letting me into their houses and/or for their insights into Roland Terry and the lasting significance of his work. Thanks also to Pat Soden of the University of Washington Press and Ed Marquand, Vivian Larkins, Marie Weiler, and the rest of the crew at Marquand Books for a relatively painless publishing ride.

ADDITIONAL PHOTOGRAPHY CREDITS

House & Garden, Feb. 1953, pp. 32–35

House & Garden, April 1958, pp. 52–55

House & Garden, Oct. 1961, p. 58

House & Garden, Aug. 1966, pp. 106–9

House & Garden, Nov. 1966, pp. 101, 103

House Beautiful, Aug. 1958, pp. 50, 51

House Beautiful, Nov. 1960, pp. 38–40, 44, 46, 110, 112

Institutions Magazine, June 1970, p. 141

Interior Design, April 1964, p. 137

Lou Hammond & Associates, Inc., p. 148

Special Collections Division, University of Washington Libraries, photo by DM:
neg. no. 4502, p. 12; neg. no. 4812, p. 14; neg. no. 4620, p. 18; neg. no. 4735, p. 19;
neg. no. 4378, p. 22; neg. no. 4382, p. 23; neg. no. 4385, p. 24; neg. no. 4383, p. 25
top right; neg. no. 4502, p. 26; neg. no. 4505, p. 27; neg. no. 5317, p. 28; neg. no.
5323, p. 29; neg. no. 5318, p. 31; neg. no. 4731, p. 41; neg. no. 4733, p. 42 left; neg.
no. 4725, p. 42 right; neg. no. 4732, p. 43; neg. no. 4474, p. 45; neg. no. 4471, p. 46
bottom; neg. no. 4469, p. 47; neg. no. 4814, p. 48; neg. no. 4801, p. 49; neg. no. 4816,
p. 51; neg. no. 4592, p. 56; neg. no. 4603, p. 57; neg. no. 4588, p. 58; neg. no. 4587,
p. 59; neg. no. 4566, p. 70; neg. no. 4891, p. 72; neg. no. 4647, p. 74; neg. no. 4648,
p. 76; neg. no. 4644, p. 77; neg. no. 4784, p. 81; neg. no. 4401, p. 133